MERCY, RANSOM, REDEMPTION

MERCY, RANSOM, REDEMPTION

The Mercedarian Order and Their Mission to Set the Captives Free

By Larry Peterson

CATHOLIC TREEHOUSE, COLUMBUS, OHIO 2024

Mercy, Ransom, Redemption: The Mercedarian Order and Their Mission to
Set the Captives Free

ISBN 979-8-9855509-9-3

Copyright © 2024 by Catholic Treehouse.

This work has been prayerfully entrusted to the patronage of Our Lady of Mercy.

Dedication

To all the many kind, gentle, and holy priests who always have remained true to their faith and vocation and have been and continue to be shining examples for so many, *God bless you all.*

And I will raise up for myself a faithful priest,
who shall do according to what is in my heart and in my mind;
and I will build him a sure house,
and he shall go in and out before my anointed for ever.

1 Samuel 2:35

Table of Content

Acknowledgements 3

Introduction 5

Our Lady of Ransom 7

The Charism of the Order of Mercy 9

Fr. Daniel Bowen O. de M.
    Director of Mercedarian Vocations USA 11

The Love Story That Required a Priest 15

Fr. Scottston Brentwood O. de M. 19

The Redemption of Michael Highfield 23

Hope Sanford, Third Order Mercedarian 41

The Queen of Martyrs Saves a "Gangbanger" 43

Fr. Anthony Fortunato O. de M. 49

St. Peter Nolasco
    Founder of the Mercedarians 51

Fr. Matthew Phelan O. de M. 55

St. Maria de Cervellón 57

Fr. Pasquale Rosca O. de M. 59

The First Mercedarians in the USA 61

Fr. Eugene Costa O. de M. 65

Our Lady of Bonaria and
    the Miracle of the Chest Lost at Sea 67

Ms. Anne DeSantis
    Director of the Raymond Nonnatus Foundation 71

Table of Content

Fr. Juan Gilberto-Jofre and Our Lady of the Forsaken..............................75

Fr. Kenneth Breen O. de M. 79

Blessed Mariana of Jesus Navarro 85

Fr. Michael Donovan O. de M. 89

Brother Matthew Levis O. de M. 93

A Mercedarian Walks Into a Diner..95

St. Peter Paschal 97

Fr. David Spencer O. de M..101

St. Raymond Nonnatus...105

Fr. Joseph Eddy O. de M. 109

Servant of God Antonino Pisano...115

Brother Raymond Colombaro O. de M..121

St. Serapion of Algiers 123

Fr. Justin Freeman O. de M. 125

Martyrs of the Spanish Civil War 127

Fr. Oscar Z. Kozyra O. de M. 129

Kevin Cush Mercedarian Postulant..133

Fr. James Mayer O. de M..137

Our Lady of Mercy: Mother and Foundress of
    the Order of the Blessed Virgin Mary of Mercy.......................................143

Mercedarian Vocation Overview 145

Epilogue...149

Contacts...151

Acknowledgements

Several key people supported me as this book was written. They deserve not only acknowledgment but also my sincere thanks and appreciation. They are:

- Fr. Daniel Bowen. O. de M., Mercedarian Vocation Director USA: I was honored and humbled to be entrusted with the task of writing this book. Learning about the Mercedarians was a life changing experience.
- Ms. Diane Hosman; Editor: her keen eye and editing skills were invaluable.
- Hope Sanford; Third Order Mercedarian: Hope kept me updated on changes within the order as they occurred since the Mercedarians are always on the move.
- Lisa-Faith McAlpine: I shall always be grateful to Lisa for sharing the story of her husband Michael's redemption.
- Lastly, I want to thank all Mercedarians who took the time and effort to send me their written vocation stories This work could never have been done without your cooperation.

If I have overlooked or missed someone in these acknowledgments, I apologize. I do, however, thank everyone involved in this project for heeding the call of Jesus and the Blessed Mother and continuing the fight for the redemption of souls.

God bless you all,
Larry Peterson

Introduction

I live in the Tampa Bay area on the Florida west coast, in a town called Pinellas Park. We border St. Petersburg and our parish name is Sacred Heart. I had never heard of or seen a Mercedarian priest. That was about to change.

During the month of May, 2014, a young Mercedarian priest was assigned to our parish. His name was Fr. Scottson Brentwood. We would quickly get to know him as Fr. Scott. He was 31 years old and had been ordained to the holy priesthood in July of 2012.

I remember standing near the church entrance when I saw Father Scott for the first time. He was wearing the traditional white Mercedarian habit, which included the crowning addition of a black *Saturno* hat. The hat is called a *Saturno* because it has a rounded top and wide brim which circles the wearer's head. It looks like a mini version of the planet Saturn. It was an inspiring sight to behold as Fr. Scott walked across the parking lot towards the church. I thought I was looking into an old viewfinder and taking a peek back into the Middle Ages. Father Scott quickly became a part of our parish Family.

A few years passed and Fr. Scott was transferred to the Monastery of Our Lady of Mercy in Philadelphia. Another Mercedarian priest replaced him. His name was Fr. Daniel Bowen. Father Daniel has a fascinating story. He was raised as a Jehovah's Witness and was a convert to Catholicism. He is presently the Vocation Director for the Mercedarians, and he has been hoping and praying for this book to become a reality.

After getting to know both of these men. I could not help but think that if they were representative of our Church's future, that future was as bright as a morning sun.

The members of this Order are called Mercedarians. The full name is "The Order of the Blessed Virgin Mary of Mercy." Besides taking the vows of poverty, chastity, and obedience, these people take a fourth vow. They take the Vow of Redemption. They pledge to trade their lives for anyone in danger of losing theirs. There are many Mercedarians who have lovingly paid the ultimate sacrifice to save another.

This book is not a book about religion. It is a storybook about people who found a calling to become part of a religious order. The people you will meet had a connecting denominator that has been their lynchpin since their founding in 1218 by St. Peter Nolasco. For eight centuries they have all found Jesus, came to love him, and chose to spend their lives in service to him. They still even wear those magnificent white habits.

In professing the Rule of St. Augustine and in seeking the perfection of love which the fourth vow requires, members cultivate a union of heart, spirit, and goods by creating a climate of friendship and mutual affection. They share what this union brings and use it for their redemptive mission.

By living in common they experience the faith and prayer that they express in their particular lifestyle. They bear each other's burdens, accept and love one another's similarities and differences, and are always ready to pardon each other's offenses.

Maybe you feel an ongoing tug inside you. Maybe it is time to pay attention to it. Perhaps Jesus has chosen you and is trying to get your attention. Man or woman, it does not matter. He loves us all.

Our Lady of Ransom

What does it mean to ransom? To ransom means to obtain the release of a prisoner by payment of exchange. Applied to our faith, we read in 1 Timothy 2:5-6: "For there is one God, and there is one mediator between God and men, the man Christ Jesus, who gave himself as a ransom for all, the testimony to which was borne at the proper time." Overall, the understanding of this passage is that the language of "payment" and "ransom" is a metaphorical way of saying that Christ has done all things necessary to save and redeem mankind enslaved.

The Feast of Our Lady of Ransom began principally in the 13th century. The Blessed Mother, Our Lady of Ransom, appeared separately to St. Peter Nolasco, his confessor St. Raymond of Penafort, and King James I of Aragon, all on the night of August 1, 1218. She urged for the creation of a religious order to carry out this task of perfect charity: helping the captives.

The Order of Mercy was subsequently established by the King on August 10th. Their chief duties included gathering alms for ransom, guarding the coasts against captors, and even giving themselves up in exchange for the release of others. This included dying for a Christian in danger of losing his faith. Indeed, their fourth vow in their constitution—after poverty, chastity, and obedience—states that Mercedarians are "to visit and to free Christians who are in captivity and in the power of the Saracens or of other enemies of our Law... By this work of mercy... all the brothers of this Order, as sons of true obedience, must always be gladly disposed to give up their lives, if it is necessary, as Jesus Christ gave up his for us."

The Mercedarian Order kept up their holy and pious work for years, celebrating its feast day on the first Sunday after August 1. It was later changed to September 24. The Order was formalized by Pope Gregory IX. Soon, the feast day spread to celebrations in Spain and France. Pope Innocent XII included the feast for the entire Church in the liturgical calendar in the 17th century. It is estimated that during this time, nearly 500,000 were saved by ransom.

We can beseech Our Lady of Ransom today to aid the suffering of those still in captivity in other lands, as well as interceding for the end of slavery in the world in all forms – including the slavery of sin.

♛ *Feast Day: September 24*

The Charism of the Order of Mercy

Merriam-Webster defines "charism" as "an extraordinary power given a Christian by the Holy Spirit for the good of the church."

The Charism of the Order of the Blessed Virgin Mary of Mercy distinguishes its members from other religious institutes. To fulfill their mission, Mercedarians, impelled by love, consecrate themselves to God with a special vow, by which they promise to give up their lives, as Christ gave his life for us, should it be necessary. They pledge to save those Christians who find themselves in extreme danger of losing their faith by new forms of captivity. They vow: "To visit and free those Christian captives who, by circumstances contrary to the dignity of the human person, find themselves in danger of losing their faith." As such, this vow, taken as a voluntary, conscious, and absolute promise, is characteristic of the Order. It inspires all the actions of its redemptive work and qualifies the fulfillment of their mission within the Church.

New Forms of Captivity

The new forms of captivity, which constitute the proper field of the mission and fourth vow of the Mercedarians, occur where there is a social situation that contains the following conditions:

• It is oppressive and degrading to the human person,
• It springs from principles and systems opposed to the Gospel,

- It puts the faith of Christians in danger,
- It offers the possibility of helping, visiting, and redeeming people in such situations.

So please flip the page and enter the world where love abounds, and courage confronts the most unimaginable hate. Come meet the Mercedarians.

Fr. Daniel Bowen O. de M.
Director of Mercedarian Vocations USA

I was born and raised in Mayfield Heights, an east-side suburb of Cleveland, Ohio, the middle son of three boys born to Albert and Jean Bowen. Many of you may be surprised to learn that I am a convert to Catholicism. With Fr. Francis Van Bergen, I completed my RCIA catechesis. I was baptized, confirmed, and received First Holy Eucharist (a.k.a. received into the Church) on Easter Vigil 1994 at St. Gregory the Great parish, South Euclid, Ohio. I will never forget that glorious evening. It is also why the Easter Vigil Mass is still my favorite Mass of the year.

Sadly, like so many who do not take their faith seriously or take it for granted, I stopped going to church within a few short years of that great occasion. Thankfully, our Lord never gave up on me. Through many friends and situations, God kept sending me invitations to return to an active faith relationship with him.

Finally, on Easter 2003, empty and alone, I finally was awakened from my selfish brokenness and simply let God love me. Following a youth retreat I made in the summer of 2003, I received the Sacrament of Reconciliation. This was after many years of not doing so. Finally I was set free and returned to the regular reception of the Most Holy Eucharist.

Following that great renewal of my faith in 2003, I began to see the importance of always putting my faith and faith community first in my life. This renewed love of my relationship with Jesus Christ and the Church he founded gave me the desire to become involved in the many fantastic opportunities in my home parish.

These opportunities to give back to God for all he has done for me included becoming a member of the Holy Name Society and Catholic men's fellowship. I served as a lector, an Extraordinary Minister of Holy Communion, and a volunteer at the pizza-sausage booth during my home parish's annual summer festival. I also became a daily Communicant. The profound blessings of going to daily Mass really should be known by all.

It was later in that same year and through my growing love of God and neighbor that I began to experience and eventually respond to a call to the priesthood and religious life. Following two years of discernment, in August 2006, I left my career, possessions, friends, and family and entered the Order of the Blessed Virgin Mary of Mercy.

On July 9, 2008, in the Chapel of St. Raymond Nonnatus in Mercygrove, Le Roy, New York, the Church received my first simple vows to God and to the Order of Mercy of chastity, poverty, obedience, and redemption. These vows are called "simple" because they are temporary and must be renewed annually. The vows are renewed for three to nine years to allow ample time to discern the calling, at which time one professes solemn, perpetual vows that are permanent and life-long.

In May 2013, after completing six years of philosophy and theology studies for the priesthood, I was granted a master of divinity, and a master of arts degree from St. Charles Borromeo Seminary in Philadelphia, Pennsylvania. God is so good!

While in Philadelphia, I resided with my brother friars at the Monastery of Our Lady of Mercy. This is the house of studies for our religious community in the United States. It was then that I was given the assignment of Director of Religious Education at Our Lady of Mercy— St. Brigid Parish, and moved from Philadelphia to Le Roy, New York.

While being Director of Religious Education, I continued my discernment with the Mercedarians and my calling to the holy priesthood. On May 6, 2014, at Our Lady of Mercy Parish in Le Roy, New York, I professed my solemn, perpetual vows to God and to the Order of Mercy of chastity, poverty, obedience, and redemption. In November 2014 I was ordained to the transitional diaconate by Bishop Edward Grosz, the auxiliary bishop of the Diocese of Buffalo.

Finally, by the grace of God, on Saturday, August 15, 2015—the Solemnity of the Assumption of the Blessed Virgin Mary—I was ordained a priest in my home parish of Sacred Heart of Jesus (formerly St. Gregory the Great) by Bishop Richard Lennon of Cleveland, Ohio.

My entire journey thus far has been to receive the most wonderful gifts. I really cannot put into words all that my vocation means to me, other than to say that I am eternally grateful. I love being a Mercedarian priest. I thank God for everything, especially for our Blessed Mother, and the saints. I thank all my beloved friends in Christ for all the prayers and support that allows me to be a good, faithful and holy priest, a servant to God's servants. It helps me to free the captives joyfully and assist them to embrace all that our Almighty God desires for us. May we always bring the joy of the Gospel to everyone we meet.

The Love Story That Required a Priest

Every once in a while, God gives you a glimpse into his heart, and the pride you have in knowing him explodes inside you. The following is a true story, and I—the author—witnessed it. Ever since it happened, it has been a part of me. It is, foremost, a love story, a love story surely inspired by God himself. And it was a Mercedarian priest who brought this nonfiction tale to its spiritual conclusion.

It was the spring of 2014. Ed and Cathy Carmello had only been my neighbors for a short time, less than a year, but we had become good friends. They had met when Ed was 60 and Cathy was 40. They fell in love and, never having been married, happily "tied the knot." Having just celebrated their silver wedding anniversary, they were enjoying retired life together.

There was a problem. Ed's prostate cancer had returned with a vengeance, had spread into his bone, and was destroying him quickly. Cathy had been diagnosed with Stage IV melanoma. She told me about her diagnosis when she had maybe six months to live.

Since I was a prostate cancer survivor and my first wife had died of melanoma, they felt comfortable discussing their cancers with me. They knew I understood. Although I tried to hide it, my heart was breaking for them. They could sense my emotions and wanted to make me smile.

Cathy offered me an Easter cookie she had made. It worked. I did smile as I bit into it.

My daily routine usually starts at around five-thirty in the morning with a two-mile walk. For some reason, on this particular day, I decided to take another walk. It was on a Thursday afternoon around four in the afternoon. I tried to talk myself out of taking this walk, but I kept feeling I had to do it. I listened to my gut and headed down the street.

Cathy and Ed's house was three down from mine. Ed had a Ford pickup with a cap on the bed. As I passed the truck, I saw Cathy standing on her front lawn supported by her walker. I could see she was fighting to hold herself up. A bit anxious, I hurried over and said, "Hey, Cathy, what are you doing? Is everything all right?"

"I was waiting for you, Larry. I need to talk to you."

I was dumbfounded. "Are you kidding me? I never walk at this time of day, and you say you were waiting for me?"

"I just knew you were coming by. I can't explain it."

There are times when things happen that are unexplainable. This was one of them. I had a chill run down my back. I really did. I leaned against the pickup as she leaned heavily on her walker. "You know Ed is dying, right?"

"Yes, Cathy, I know. We talked about it. What about your prognosis? Any change?"

She smiled, looked me right in the eye, and said, "They told me I only have a few weeks left."

I tightened my lips, took a breath, and asked, "What can I do?"

They knew that I was Catholic and an Extraordinary Minister of Holy Communion (EMHC). She told me that they had been non-practicing

Catholics and had not been to church in years. Then she asked me if I could bring a priest over. It was time for them to "make things right with God." I said, "I will put a call into Father as soon as I get back to the house."

"Thank you so much. That is why I was out there waiting for you."

I simply nodded. She smiled and thanked me, then asked me to come in and see Ed. We slowly walked back to her house. She did not mention herself once, only her husband. She told me how she wished she could ease his suffering and how wonderful it might be if they could go for a bicycle ride just one more time. Then she mentioned how she thanked God for every moment they had had together.

I went inside and Cathy, Ed, and I hung out for about ten minutes just chatting. Cathy excused herself and slowly walked back to the bedroom. Ed quickly told me how he wished he could ease her suffering and how God had been so good to him, allowing him to find such a great woman with whom to share his life. I took in a deep breath. I was witnessing marital love in its purest form. And since God is Love, you know when God is present. At that moment, it was hard for me to breathe.

I called our newly ordained priest, a Mercedarian friar, Fr. Scott. He came over the next day and spent the better part of the afternoon with Ed and Cathy. Ed and the young priest both had roots in Roanoke, Virginia, and talked and laughed and had a raucous good time together. Although separated by more than 50 years, it did not matter. It was as if they had grown up together. It was beautiful.

Father heard their confessions, anointed each of them, and gave them Holy Communion. Sunday was Palm Sunday. It was the beginning of Holy Week, and Father would be busy. He told them he would come back as soon as he could. They all hugged and said goodbye. On Palm Sunday, I had the honor of bringing them Holy Communion.

Easter Sunday, I was privileged to bring Ed and Cathy Holy Communion again. They were lying next to each other in bed, holding hands. Ed smiled and said, "Larry, we are so happy. This is the greatest Easter we have ever had."

He turned and looked at his wife, who was smiling lovingly at him. She reached over and wiped his wet, tear-soaked cheeks. They stared into each other's eyes, and I thought they were maybe looking into each other's souls. It was a moment filled with a shared spirituality I had never witnessed before. I could feel it. I do not doubt that at that moment, Jesus was there, with them, holding their hands in his.

The lynchpin in this redemption moment had been the Mercedarian priest. Sealed with the Sacrament of Holy Orders, Fr. Scott Brentwood O. de M. had brought those gifts to Ed and Cathy a few days before Palm Sunday. He had heard their confessions, anointed them, and given them Holy Communion. You could sense the presence of God's grace flowing throughout the house. Ed and Cathy were ready to leave on their final journey.

As for me, I thank God for their friendship and for being a part of their final journey. The love they shared together and the peace and joy in their hearts as they knowingly approached the end of their lives on earth, was beautiful to watch. I was blessed to have been a witness to such a beautiful love story. Having a Mercedarian priest present was a wondrous thing. Embracing the priceless gift of faith can be like an explosion of magnificent rainbows surrounding you. Faith is there for all of us, if we so choose.

Ed died the week after Easter. A week after his funeral Mass, Cathy moved into a hospice house. Her nephew, home on leave from the air force for his uncle's funeral, accompanied her. She lived another two weeks. Sometimes I wonder if couples can ride bicycles together in heaven. If the answer is "yes," I can see Ed and Cathy riding along, side by side, smiling from ear to ear.

Fr. Scottston Brentwood O. de M.

I spent my early years in the mountains of Virginia in a little corner of the world that still maintains a unique atmosphere of tranquility and lack of modernization all along the Blue Ridge Parkway. We had everything from trees to open fields—as rustic as one can get—but a community that was very aware of its codependence on one another. Everyone knew everyone, and the stereotype of "small-town life" very much applied. The best comparison I can make is Mayberry from the *Andy Griffith Show*, which is a twenty-minute drive from where I lived.

Being in the "Bible Belt," faith was a powerful and present reality of everyday life. Everything started and ended with a prayer, and even when prayer in school was no longer permitted, the students still said them without the prompting of the administration. The Catholic presence, however, was minimal and almost nonexistent. In my house, religion was important, but not too important. We were not as religious as other families, but I would not say it was lacking. We said our prayers before and after meals and before we went to bed, but it was not a major part of my growing up.

I began to consider a vocation to be a priest when I was fourteen. I was working at a government institution where the government distributes assistance to people who are poor. Before I worked there, I thought most people only abused the program. I thought they did not need the help but took it because it was available. When I worked there, I discovered that this was true. One time, however, I helped a family that really needed help. Afterward, I tried to find a way to help others in more than just material ways.

At the time, I did not know about religious life, and my only real understanding of priestly life was that of the diocese. When I was seventeen, I decided I would pursue a priestly vocation. I talked with the vocation director for the diocese of Virginia. He told me that the diocese does not accept anyone until they have graduated from a university.

I went to Old Dominion University. It is a large university of 30,000 students. I made many friends, and some of these friends also wanted to pursue a vocation to the priesthood or religious life. When I learned about religious life, I felt that this was what God wanted for me. I liked the idea of living together with others who wanted to work for the same cause. I investigated different religious congregations, but I did not find any I wanted to join.

During my last year at the university, a friend of mine visited the Mercedarians. When he returned, he told me I should visit them. I said no. I did not want to spend more time looking at congregations because I had looked at them before and did not see any that I liked. That September, a hurricane came to Norfolk, the city of my university. Everyone was evacuated from the university. My family was eight hours away, so it was impossible for me to go home.

I asked the same friend if I could stay with him in his apartment downtown. He said I could but told he was leaving to be with his family, so I stayed in his apartment alone. The electricity died the first day, and the only activities I could do were study biology, pray, and look at the walls. I spent more time looking at the walls than I did studying or praying.

My friend visited many different communities. When he visited these communities, he always took cards of their saints so he could remember to pray for the communities. He would put them in the edges of other pictures. When I was looking at these images, the images for the Mercedarians seemed different. I thought I would call them and ask some questions I had. I did not want to visit because the closest house was in Philadelphia, and Philadelphia was eight hours from my university by car.

When I finally called, I asked many questions. I was happy with the answers, so I visited the following November. I returned to Philadelphia the next January before returning to my university. For my break in the spring, I returned to Philadelphia to complete the testing necessary for the application. I graduated from my university in May and entered the Mercedarians in August.

Deacon Scottston Brentwood was ordained to the Holy Priesthood by Most Reverend Bishop Joseph Francis Martino on September 4, 2012, at Our Lady of Lourdes Church in Overbrook, Pennsylvania. He now bears the title of Fr. Scottston Brentwood, O. de M., and he currently serves as Superior and Pastor Our Lady of Mercy and St. Brigid Parishes in Leroy, New York.

The Redemption of Michael Highfield

T his is a story about a man who was lost and wanted to be found. Facing certain death from a demon called lung cancer, he reached out to a stranger, asking for help. The stranger's name was God, and the man was asking for a new life. Was it too late for a man who had led a life of self-gratification, a life of abusing and stealing from others, a life filled with sinfulness?

This man discovered that his prayers for help would be answered in ways he could never have imagined. A Mercedarian priest, a member of the Order of the Blessed Virgin Mary of Mercy, would come to him and lead him on his journey. That pilgrimage would lead to a place called Love. The man would discover that he knew Love all along. That Love would be God.

Sacred Heart Catholic Church is on the northern borderline of St. Petersburg, Florida, in Pinellas Park. As one of their active ministries, Sacred Heart has Extraordinary Ministers of Holy Communion, also known as EMHCs. These volunteers assist the priests by distributing Holy Communion at Mass and by bringing Communion to the sick and the homebound. Tom McCabe is a parishioner who serves on this ministry. He has done so for many years.

Tom's weekly stops included Northside Hospital in St. Petersburg. Sometime in the middle of September 2017, while making one of those visits, a nurse stopped him in the hallway. "Excuse me, sir, I have a request from a patient."

A bit surprised at being stopped by a nurse, Tom answered, "Sure, what is it?"

"There is a man in room 343 who asked me to ask you to stop in and see him."

"Sure thing, no problem. Do you know what the man wants?"

"He told me he needed to talk to a priest. He saw the cross you were wearing, so he asked to see you."

"Well, I am not a priest. I bring Holy Communion to the patients who request it. That's all I do. But I will stop and see him before I leave."

The nurse smiled at Tom and said, "Thank you. His name is Michael."

She walked away, and Tom McCabe stood still for a moment thinking.

He did not know what to expect from this person. He was not even sure if the man was Catholic. He blessed himself, said a silent prayer for some wisdom, and headed to room 343. He paused a few feet from the entrance and took a deep breath. Then he walked in. There was an empty bed near the doorway and another across the room near the window. The man in the window bed said, "Hello Father, thank you for stopping. I appreciate it. "

Tom slowly walked over to the man and said, "You're Michael, right? The nurse said you wanted to see me." The man nodded, and Tom continued, "Nice to meet you. My name is Tom, and I am from Sacred Heart Catholic Church, but I am not a priest. I bring Holy Communion to the patients here. But I will help you any way I can."

Michael, getting a bit nervous, said, "Look, I saw you wearing that Cross, and I thought you were a priest. I want to see a priest. I have stage four lung cancer, and I am dying. I got to get right with God. Can you help me get a priest? Please."

Sensing the urgency in Michael's voice, Tom said, "Sure, Michael, I will call Father, and I'm sure he will come to see you."

"Look Tom, I have to get Baptized. I got to become a Catholic. I have done many bad things in my life, and I need forgiveness before it is too late. And I know you Catholics have the real thing."

Tom was taken back and looked at Michael without saying anything. Michael said, "What's the matter? Is something wrong?"

Tom shrugged a bit and said, "You used the words, 'real thing.' I'm curious, what did you mean by that?"

"You know, the real thing. Jesus in the bread. The priest turns bread into the body of Jesus during Mass, and it is the real thing. And then the people get to receive him. I want to receive him so bad. I heard about it in prison."

Tom realized he was referring to the Real Presence, Christ being truly present in the Holy Eucharist under the appearance of bread and wine. It is a fundamental teaching and dogma of the Catholic Faith, and Michael Highfield learned about it in prison. Tom was dumbfounded. Many self-professed Catholics did not believe this truth, and here was this unbaptized, non-Christian ex-convict, knowing about the Real Presence.

Tom got close to the bed and said, "Can I say a prayer with you, Michael? Then I will leave and talk to Fr. Daniel. He will come to see you. That is the man you need to speak to."

Michael asked, "I have been in prison. Is that a problem?"

"Of course not, Michael. Jesus is all about forgiveness. That is not an issue."

Michael said, "Ok, that is great. When folks hear I was in prison it sometimes does not go well for me."

Tom smiled and said, "Not a problem. Don't worry about that at all."

"Now look," Michael replied, "I am counting on you. You won't forget, will you?"

Tom said, "I promise you, I will not forget. I understand how important this is. Now let's bow our heads, and we will pray together."

They both bowed their heads, and Tom quietly said a prayer asking God's protection for Michael. He said goodbye to Michael and headed out to the hallway. He pulled out his cell phone and dialed Fr. Daniel Bowen. Tom left a message for the priest and then walked to the elevator. His work at Northside finished, he was headed home. But, it would not be his last day visiting Michael Highfield.

The next day, Fr. Daniel Bowen, O. de M., went to Northside Hospital to visit Michael Highfield. The Mercedarians wear their traditional white habits when out in public. When Father walked into Michael's room, the sick man just stared, unblinking with his mouth hanging open as Father approached his bed. He could not believe what he was seeing. "Hi Michael, I'm Fr. Bowen, Fr. Daniel Bowen. You can call me Fr. Daniel. My friend, Tom, told me you asked to see a priest." He held out his hands and laughingly said, "Well, you are looking at one." Father Daniel was raised as a Jehovah's Witness, converted to Catholicism, and had become a Mercedarian priest. He not only loved his faith, but he was also passionate about it.

Michael was nervous and had never dealt with or been involved with a Catholic priest in his entire life. His mother, a Catholic woman, had his siblings baptized when they were babies, but fell away from the faith. She never bothered to get Michael baptized. Except for what he had heard in prison, he had no religious background at all. Father Daniel's easy manner and smile had put Michael at ease. "Uh, hello Father, thanks so much for coming. I need to be baptized. Please baptize me."

Father Daniel said, "Hold on, Michael. I am here for you, but there is a process I must follow. I will baptize you but it will not happen today. First, we have some work to do."

The Miracle of the Reaching Hand

Michael John Highfield was born in Aurora, Illinois, on February 20, 1955. There is not much information about his childhood available. He did have three siblings and his mother had them baptized in the Catholic Church. However, for reasons unknown, she never had Michael baptized. He grew up without any religious education or background and knew very little about God. However, he did have a vivid memory of something that had happened to him when he was seven years old. This memory had always been there for him to turn to.

Michael remembers playing out front and looking up at the clouds. He had heard people talk about God and heaven, but he did not believe the stories. He was holding a stick in his hand, which was about two feet long. As he stared up at the sky, he thought of a way he could find out if God was real or make-believe. All Michael would have to do is ask God to catch the stick. Raising his head to heaven, he yelled out, "Hey God, if you are really there, catch this stick."

Seven-year-old Michael Highfield flung the stick up in the air as hard as he could. He watched, and suddenly, he witnessed a sight he would never forget. A hand reached down from the clouds. Closer and closer it came, and then, the hand opened, and the fingers wrapped around the stick and, just like that, the hand and the stick vanished into the heavens.

The little boy stared, dumbfounded, stunned, frightened and overjoyed. That mix of sudden emotions would be with him for the rest of his life. It may have been that memory that had him searching for salvation as his life was winding down. If there was one thing Michael was sure of, he knew there was a God.

It is unknown when Michael moved to Florida. Did he come with his parents or with another relative? He was in Florida when he began ninth grade, so he was too young to move there by himself. We can leave it at that. Some reports say his father had a stroke when Michael was very young and passed away. That has not been corroborated. What is known is that he made it to the ninth grade in school and dropped out: he began doing what most ninth-grade dropouts do. He started getting in trouble. Several confinements in juvenile facilities followed.

Then Michael graduated to the big time. A jury found him guilty of burglary. At 19 years old, he was sentenced to several years in prison for the crime.

Michael's Shining Star

Michael was incarcerated in prison numerous times between 1974 and his last release, on January 13, 2015. It had been a forty-year life of crime, parole, odd-jobs, and more crime. Many of his crimes involved substance abuse, both using and selling. There was one bright spot in Michael's life. God had blessed him with a special shining star. However, he would not realize until 2017 how brightly that star had shined for him over the years. That shining star had a name: Lisa.

The year was 1979, and Michael was on parole. He would find part-time jobs in the neighborhood and hang out at the Pinellas Square Mall in Pinellas Park, Florida. He managed to pick up occasional day jobs, but spent most of his time at the mall. It was a popular hang-out for teens and Michael was a grown man. A steady intake of illegal drugs combined with spending time in jail will stunt a person's emotional development. Michael Highfield was proof of this. His maturity was that of a teenager. Unfortunately, that teenage mind was living inside the body of a 24-year-old adult.

One afternoon Michael spotted a young girl walking toward him. He wasted no time in approaching her. Smitten by a grown man flirting with her, the youngster giggled and smiled at him. Their encounter would be the beginning of an on-again, off-again relationship that would last for the rest of Michael's life.

Lisa was fourteen years old and immediately attracted to Michael. She began to miss school to meet him at a 7-11, the park, or the mall. Lisa's absences from school and failing grades quickly made her parents realize their daughter was getting into trouble. They were unsure what kind of trouble, but that changed the night Lisa's dad caught Michael climbing in his daughter's bedroom window. He chased the young man, but Michael was too fast and got away. At the time, her folks did not realize that Michael was a 24-year-old high school dropout and an ex-convict on parole.

Those revelations would come to them soon enough. When Lisa's folks found out, they tried to stop her from seeing Michael. They went to the school and asked the guidance counselor and principal for their help. They suggested that the parents get a restraining order. School officials could keep Michael away from the school but after school was out, it was up to the parents to do their best to keep this "boyfriend" away from their daughter.

They did secure a restraining order. If caught together, Michael's parole would be violated, and he would go back to prison. Lisa's parents never saw them together, but it did not matter. Michael went back to jail anyway. It was for committing burglary... again.

And so it went for Michael and Lisa. Lisa dropped out of high school and got a job at Burger King. Most of the money she earned would be given to Michael when he was out on parole. They married, separated, lived together, separated, and did not see each other for close to twenty years. He would go back to jail, get out, and go back again. Michael and Lisa would be together, off and on, right up until the end.

January 13, 2015, was when Michael was released from prison for the last time. Cancer had started growing in his lungs, and he would need care. The one person that would be there for him was Lisa. Despite years of heartache, she cared deeply for the man and would be by his side most every day as his final journey continued.

Seeking Redemption

When Michael was released from prison, he moved in with his nephew in St. Petersburg. That only lasted a short time, and then he moved in with a friend. While in prison, cancer was growing in his lungs. By the time he went home, it was widespread. He was able to qualify for treatment at the Florida Cancer Center in St. Petersburg. The doctors at the center determined the type of cancer he had and prescribed a regimen of chemotherapy treatments, which probably began during the summer of 2015. Lisa became the person who would take him to and from his oncology and chemotherapy visits.

During the summer of 2017, an ambulance transported Michael to Northside Hospital in St. Petersburg. The pain had increased as the lung cancer continued its relentless assault on his body. He was having severe breathing problems. The hospitalizations and breathing treatments had been steady during the previous six months. Michael knew what his body was telling him, and that is why he had asked for a priest at this time. Michael Highfield had reached out to a stranger to help him bring his eternal soul to salvation. God had sent him the third blessing in his life: the Mercedarians.

After their initial meeting, Fr. Daniel was unexpectedly called out of town for several days. Unable to return to the hospital right away, he contacted a Third Order Mercedarian, Hope Sanford. Members of a religious Third Order are members of the laity and are not consecrated religious, but they have the charism of the order for which they take vows. Father Daniel asked Hope if she could go to the hospital and give Michael some instruction in the prime doctrines of the Catholic faith. Hope readily agreed.

Father Daniel called Michael and explained why he could not return for a few days. He told him that Hope, a retired teacher, would begin teaching him Catholic basics. Hope drove to the hospital, went up to Michael's room, introduced herself, and they got on as if they had known each other for years. Hope spent about an hour and a half talking to Michael about the Holy Eucharist and Jesus, forgiveness, redemption, and salvation. Michael hung on her every word. He told her that if he survived the cancer he was going to devote the rest of his life helping others.

He thanked her when she was leaving and asked when Father was coming to baptize him. She said she thought it would be on his next visit in a day or two. He had tears in his eyes as he smiled at her. They waved at each other as she left.

A few days later, Fr. Daniel called Hope and told her that he had tried to call Michael, but there was no answer. He asked her if she would try to contact him. Hope called and received no response. She then drove to Northside Hospital to see Michael. When she got to his room, she discovered he was not there. Michael's oncologist had discharged him, and the nurses on duty had no idea where he went or who had picked him up. Hope remembered from their conversation where he lived. It was only five blocks from her apartment. She called Fr. Daniel, told him the good news, and told him she was leaving right away. Father said, "Thanks Hope. Keep me posted."

Hope arrived at the house and walked up the cluttered walkway to the front door. The door was ajar, and Hope knocked while calling out, "Michael, Michael, are you in there?"

All she heard was the loud bark of a large dog. She called out again and the dog started barking louder and faster. Then she heard someone yelling, "Help me, help me... please help me."

Hope was terrified of the barking dog but she began to push open the door anyway. In the living room corner was a kennel holding a very angry pit bull. The dog was so agitated that it was making the wire kennel bounce up and down as it tried to get out and attack Hope. She had to walk past the kennel and the raging dog to get back to Michael who was hollering for help. When she got to the bedroom and he saw her he started yelling, "Baptize me, baptize me, I'm dying, I'm dying."

Hope, bombarded with the hysterics coming from a raging pit bull and a sick man, called 911. It was a reflexive move but the right one. Michael was still yelling for her to baptize him and the dog was still barking when Hope's phone rang. It was Fr. Daniel trying to find out if she had found Michael at home. As she started to speak, the paramedics came hurrying in. Hope started to cry and could barely talk. Father said to Hope, "Let me speak to the paramedics."

Father asked the medic about Michael's condition. He told Fr. Daniel that Michael was stable and being transported to the hospital. Hope got back on the phone, and Father told her not to worry. They were taking Michael to the hospital. He asked her to meet him there.

Father Daniel called Tom McCabe, the EMHC who first met Michael, and asked Tom to meet him at Northside. Everything seemed to be in order except for one minor detail. The paramedics did not tell anyone they were taking Michael to St. Petersburg General Hospital and not to Northside Hospital. Father Daniel, Tom, and Hope had all gone to Northside.

Three cars pulled up to the emergency room entrance at Northside Hospital simultaneously. Hope hurried into the ER and asked if Michael Highfield had been brought in yet. She was told that Northside had no available beds, so no new patients were coming there. The nurse asked, "Could they have gone to St. Pete General?"

Father Daniel said, "We don't know. Can we call there?"

The nurse replied, "Give me a minute."

They watched as she went into the triage room and picked up the phone. A few minutes later, she came out and said, "Okay folks, Michael Highfield is at St. Pete General."

The delay was a good thing because it allowed the staff to get Michael settled in before anyone got there. Father, Tom, and Hope arrived at St. Petersburg General while the nurses were settling Michael into the emergency room. They waited in the lobby lounge for about a half-hour before a nurse came and told them they could go back to see him. When Michael saw Fr. Daniel come in he yelled out in his raspy voice, "Father, please baptize me. Please baptize me."

Father Daniel walked over to Michael's bedside and placed his hand on top of Michael's. "Don't' worry, my friend. We are going to baptize you. This is your special day."

The Baptism of Michael Highfield

Michael Highfield had been pleading to be baptized. But why? Why was he so desperate for this to happen? He had no religious background and had led a godless, self-serving, sinful life. But Michael had recognized and accepted his mortality. But why baptism? Remember the "Miracle of the Reaching Hand?" Ever since that day, Michael believed there was a God. But Michael knew nothing about God and rarely gave him a thought until this point in his life. Now Michael wanted the God he knew existed to be part of his life.

This is what Jesus Christ is all about. He loves us, each and every one of us. But we cannot see him or touch him or text him or call him. How do we get to know him? How do we know he is with us? We know because of the sacraments.

Most everyone has heard of the Good Shepherd. The Good Shepherd is Jesus. We are his sheep. It does not matter if you are a religious person or not. Jesus is always reaching out to everyone through signs. A sacrament is defined as an "outward sign instituted by Christ to give grace."

An example of how we all receive graces from Jesus is Michael. His first "sign" was as a seven-year-old, and it was miraculous. He threw the stick up, a hand reached down from the clouds, and grabbed it. The hand holding the stick vanished into the heavens. The seven-year-old just stared and stared. Did it really happen? Was he daydreaming? It does not matter. It was a sign for the boy, making him believe in God.

It was followed by him learning about the Sacrament of Baptism while in prison. Those two moments in his life empowered him to seek out a Catholic priest as he approached the end of his life. The Good Shepherd had taken care of another seemingly "lost" sheep.

In Ezekiel 34:11 we read: "For thus says the Lord God: Behold, I, I myself will search for my sheep, and will seek them out." And in Ezekiel 34:15-17 it says: "I myself will be the shepherd of my sheep, and I will make them lie down, says the Lord God. I will seek the lost, and I will bring back the strayed, and I will bind up the crippled, and I will strengthen the weak, and the fat and the strong I will watch over; I will feed them in justice. As for you, my flock, thus says the Lord God: Behold, I judge between sheep and sheep, rams and he-goats."

Michael had been receiving graces from God and he knew that something was missing inside of him. That emptiness reached down into his soul, and he knew he must fill that void no matter what. We Catholics call the life within our souls sanctifying grace. Although he did not know it, Michael wanted that sanctifying grace. Not having it was the cause of his emptiness. When he saw Tom McCabe, who was wearing a cross, he immediately requested that Tom see him. Tom came to him and followed up his visit by contacting Fr. Daniel Bowen. Father Daniel visited Michael and began the process of bringing him into the church. This is a perfect example of Jesus taking care of one of his lost sheep.

There are seven Sacraments in the Catholic Church: Baptism, Reconciliation (Penance), Holy Eucharist, Confirmation, Holy Orders, Anointing of the Sick (Last Rites), and Matrimony. Jesus instituted them all while he was on earth. At the Last Supper, he instituted the Sacrament of Holy Eucharist and Holy Orders. He did this within the framework of the first Mass. When an ordained priest says Mass or performs other priestly duties, he stands *in persona Christi,* which is Latin for "in the person of Christ." Father Daniel was *in persona Christi* as he prepared to baptize Michael Highfield.

Tom McCabe and Hope Sanford were present in the emergency room and standing by Michael's bedside. Tom was to be the godparent and Hope a witness. Father, wearing a white stole representing new life, said, "Okay, Michael, we are about to begin. I will ask you a few questions. Just answer them with an 'I do' or an 'I am.' Are you ready?"

Michael, lips held tightly together, shook his head up and down.

Father began, "Dear Brother Michael, you have asked to be baptized because you wish to have eternal life. This is eternal life: to know the one true God and Jesus Christ, whom He has sent. This is the faith of Christians. Do you acknowledge this?"

Michael hesitated, and Father held out his hands, signaling him to respond. Michael nodded and said, "Okay, sorry... yes, I do."

Fr Daniel, read several other prayers from his book. Then he turned to Tom McCabe, the godparent, and asked, "As his godparent do you promise to remind him of it and help him learn the teachings of Christ?"

Tom answered, "I do."

Father Daniel then turned to Hope and asked, "Will you, Hope, who has witnessed this promise, assist him in fulfilling it?"

Hope answered, "I will."

Father now turned to Michael and said, "Therefore, you will now be baptized into eternal life in accordance with the command of our Lord Jesus Christ."

The head of the bed was raised higher, so Michael was almost sitting up. Father placed a white towel around Michael's neck and asked him to bow his head slightly. Michael did, and Father took the small jar holding water and said, "Michael, I baptize you in the name of the Father..."—he poured water on his head—"and of the Son..."—he poured water a second time—"and of the Holy Spirit," and he poured water a third time.

Father anointed Michael with chrism oil and said several other prayers. The ceremony was concluded when Fr. Daniel gave the blessing to Michael by making the sign of the cross with his arm and hand while saying, "May the blessing of almighty God, the Father, and the Son, and the Holy Spirit, come upon you and remain with you forever. Amen."

Michael remained in St. Petersburg General for two days. When a bed became available at Northside Hospital, his doctor transferred him there. He spent a week or so as a patient in Northside, but his condition was deteriorating. At the beginning of October, he was moved again. This time it was to Suncoast Hospice Center.

Lisa, who had been visiting him each day at Northside, was waiting for him at the entrance when the ambulance pulled up. She went over to him, rubbed her hand over his head, and squeezed his hand. Then she stepped away from the gurney as the aides pushed him into his new room and final home.

Michael's conversion to Catholicism was not yet complete. His baptism had been the first step. He still would receive the Sacraments of Reconciliation—also known as Penance or Confession—and Holy Eucharist... his First Holy Communion where he would receive "the real thing" he desperately wanted. Father Daniel would be coming to hospice to administer these sacraments. Father would make sure that Michael would not leave this world without having them.

Father Daniel, Hope Sanford, and Tom McCabe were informed of Michael's transfer to hospice. Father had time available on Friday morning, and so did Hope. Tom McCabe had a medical appointment and was unavailable. Father and Hope met at hospice at ten in the morning. Having spent the night, Lisa, was already there.

Unable to be at the baptism, it was the first time she had met Hope and Fr. Daniel. Hope, a kind, caring woman, immediately embraced Lisa, and the two quickly bonded. Lisa then gave Father a strong embrace and looked him in the eye. Tears welled up in her eyes and slid down her cheeks. "Thank you Father," she said. "You have given Michael the redemption he so desperately wanted. God bless you."

Father Daniel smiled at her and said, "No Lisa, it was not me. It was Jesus who used me as an instrument of his love. Without Jesus, there is no priesthood. Thank him." Lisa then led them to Michael's room.

With Hope and Lisa standing by, Fr. Daniel completed Michael's initiation into the Catholic Church. First, he administered the Sacrament of Confirmation to Michael. Usually only a bishop can do this but in special cases, such as Michael's, the priest is permitted to administer it. He laid his hands on Michael's head saying, "All-powerful God, Father of our Lord Jesus Christ, by water and the Holy Spirit you freed your son from sin and gave him new life. Send your Holy Spirit upon him to be his helper and guide. Give him the spirit of wisdom and understanding, the spirit of right judgment and courage, the spirit of knowledge and reverence. Fill him with the spirit of wonder and awe in your presence." Then Father dipped his right thumb in chrism and made the sign of the cross on Michael's forehead. As he did this he said, "Michael, be sealed with the gift of the Holy Spirit."

Michael answered, "Amen."

Father then led them all in saying the Lord's Prayer. When they were finished, Father turned to the table on his right. He had placed a white cloth on it and on the cloth was a lit candle and next to it was a small gold container—called a pyx—used for carrying the Holy Eucharist. He opened the pyx and removed the consecrated host from it. Holding it up for those present, he said, "This is the lamb of God, who takes away the sins of the world, happy are those who are called to this supper."

Michael had been instructed to respond in this manner: "Lord, I am not worthy to receive you, but only say the word and I shall be healed." He responded perfectly. Father, still holding the host up, approached Michael and said, "The Body of Christ."

Michael answered, "Amen." Then he opened his mouth and took the host onto his tongue.

Father prayed, "May the Lord Jesus Christ protect you and lead you to eternal life." Father Daniel, head bowed, stepped back a few steps and remained quiet. Hope and Lisa followed his lead and did the same thing. After several moments Father raised his head and said, "Congratulations, Michael, you are officially a full member of the Catholic Church. This is a great day. And thank you for allowing me to be part of your journey to Christ. It has been my honor."

Michael, realizing what had transpired, began to cry. Lisa went over to him and hugged him. The man who had led a life of virtual perdition had seized upon the graces God had sent him and embraced redemption. And it was a Mercedarian priest—a man who had vowed to give his life to save a soul if necessary—who was the one who guided him along on his redemptive journey, along with a lay Mercedarian who shared the same charism. Perhaps it is a charism you have too.

Michael Highfield was terminally ill. Each day he slid closer and closer to death. Lisa, still in love with the man who had caused her so much heartache and grief during their turbulent years together, was with him day after day. She would feed him, wash his body down, massage his feet, brush his remaining hair and be the most attentive caregiver anyone could have hoped for. She would go home for a shower and a change of clothes, and after a bit of house cleaning, she came right back to hospice. There was a lounge chair she used to sleep in, and that was it. Hope Sanford came by almost every day to assist Lisa. They had become great friends.

About four weeks after being admitted to hospice, Michael breathed his last. The date was November 9, 2017. Lisa was sitting by his side, and Hope was standing next to her. Father Daniel had come by a day or two earlier to anoint him one more time.

Michael had no money but it did not matter. The Diocese of St. Petersburg allowed Michael's funeral Mass to be said at the Cathedral of St, Jude. Father Daniel was the celebrant of the Mass. Michael Martz, the music director from Sacred Heart Church, volunteered his time to supply the music for the Mass. Tom McCabe said a few words about Michael when the Mass ended.

Michael's parents were buried at the Garden Sanctuary Cemetery in Seminole, Florida. Lisa started a GoFundMe page to get help with the final expenses. She raised enough to pay for the cremation and internment with his parents in Garden Sanctuary.

Michael passed from this world and into the next filled with sanctifying grace and having had the Apostolic Pardon conferred upon him. And in that, we can all see the wonder of Christ, the Son of God, suffering and dying for each and every one of us.

We all have choices to make up until the very end. Some, like Michael Highfield, respond to the graces they have received and choose life everlasting. Others choose a different path and do not—and will never—see and share in the glory of the God who created them. God forgives anyone who seeks it, no matter what they have done in their past. How sad it is so many reject it.

Hope Sanford
Third Order Mercedarian

Hope Sanford was born on August 17, 1946 in Santa Monica, California. Her dad was Polish, her mom, Irish, and Hope was the oldest of the three children. Her mom and dad were Catholic, and the children were all baptized and raised in the faith.

When Hope was three years old, circumstances forced the family to move to Pennsylvania. Hope's dad got a job in a steel mill in Pittsburgh, and the family settled in. Hope attended public school, and her mom took care of the family. She would eventually find work as an account manager.

As Hope grew from childhood to young adult, challenges and sufferings combined, and she found herself in a place of despair. But the Blessed Virgin heard Hope's cries for help. She showered her with the graces needed to remind her of Jesus's love for her. This was when she opened her heart to experience his love and mercy. Hope headed to Morehead University in Kentucky and earned a bachelor of arts degree in both education and in music. She graduated in 1968 and went on to teach in both Catholic and public schools for over thirty years.

Hope has two children, a son and a daughter. Both are married, both are firefighters, and they all live in the Tampa Bay area. Hope also has three grandchildren and two great grandchildren. One granddaughter is a nurse, the other works at the sheriff's department as a dispatcher. Her grandson is a deputy for the sheriff's department. Apparently, helping folks is a dominant genetic trait in Hope's family bloodline.

Hope retired in 2005 and says, "God continued to provide opportunities to share his love and mercy." A friend gave her a pamphlet about the Mercedarians and invited her to a meeting. She accepted the invitation and never looked back. After much prayer and discernment, Hope fulfilled the requirements for postulant and novice in 2007. Then she made her final promises, becoming a member of the Mercedarian Third Order.

Since 2008 she has worked tirelessly to help those who were marginalized, sick, poor, and emotionally and spiritually lost. These folks included abandoned women who were about to give birth, the homeless, those in hospice care, the homebound, and those in hospitals. Presently, she works to earn money to help people with food, rent, and utilities and helps support the Order's vocation mission. Of course, she is always available to offer prayer and moral support to anyone who might need it.

Hope says, "I am grateful to God for my life and for the incredible journey that he has provided for me. Thank you, Lord!"

Hope Sanford delivers groceries and meals to homebound folks and uses the money she earns to help the needy purchase necessities.

The Queen of Martyrs Saves a "Gangbanger"

I magine being a dad or mom who has not seen their nineteen-year-old son in over a year. You had worked hard as a parent to instill a value system and moral compass into your children, but your boy rebelled. He left home, and you had no idea where he was. You were heartbroken at the rejection he has shown you and the family. What's more, in addition to your wife and fourteen-year-old daughter, you have other things on your mind.

You are a respected police chief in a city of two million people. Responsible for crowd control for a major political convention scheduled in two days, the police commissioner has also asked you to coordinate the security forces on the convention center's perimeter. You have a job to do, and right now, it takes precedence over other things.

At six o'clock on the first night of the convention, protesters begin massing on the center's east side. You can see that they are well organized and plan to create mayhem. At nine o'clock the crowd numbers several thousand, and the screaming and yelling is getting intense. Suddenly, the crowd, urged on by several masked protesters, surges forward and then breaks into a charge.

Dressed in riot gear, you are standing at the front of your riot-ready police force. In your hand is a taser. One man is charging right at you when suddenly he stops short, falls to his knees, and drops his hands to his side. You hurry up to him and yank off his mask. You are stunned because you are looking down at your son. He is crying and telling you he is sorry. You lift him to you, and you hug each other. The surging crowd, witnessing this unexpected turn of events, stops and becomes quiet. The moment spreads, and chaos turns to silence.

Does that sound far-fetched? If so, let us now travel back over 700 years to a day when something similar really did happen. It may be 700 years ago, but people then were much like people now. Pride was at war against humility, greed was trying to destroy generosity, envy hated kindness, and lust was determined to vanquish chastity. When it comes to the wants, needs, and emotions God has instilled in us, they have not changed since Adam and Eve first walked the perfect world God had given them. And when it comes to family, love versus hate can sometimes tear loved ones apart. Just think of Cain and Abel.

Let us now meet one of the original Mercedarians. His name was Peter Armengol. Today he is known as St. Peter Armengol. His story is one for the ages. Indeed, as a young man, Peter was not a saint. Rather, he had rejected his family, his morality, and his faith. He had exchanged those things and become a self-centered egotist. Yet, he became a saint.

The 13th Century

The year is 1258 A.D. and Arnold Armengol was a member of the Spanish hierarchy. Arnold had provided his son, Peter, with the finest education and upbringing. But Peter had rejected all of that and fell into the secular trap of self-centeredness and arrogance. He even joined a band of criminals that preyed on people traveling up into the mountains. Peter was so good at this work he eventually became the gang leader.

His dad, part of the royal hierarchy, was asked by King James I of Aragon to lead him on a journey to Montpellier to meet with France's king. The king had heard of the brigands that preyed on mountain travelers and asked Arnold to provide security and lead the king and his cortege on the journey.

As Arnold Armengol led the King's entourage through the mountain passes, they were attacked by a band of highwaymen. The bandits charged toward them and Armengol quickly prepared for a counter-attack. With his sword drawn, he headed directly to the leader of the pack. They were about to engage each other when the robber fell to his knees. He had recognized his father and, with tears streaming down his face, prostrated himself at his dad's feet and handed over his sword. Peter knew that the penalty for his crimes was death, but at that moment, he did not care.

Imprisoned in Barcelona, Peter Armengol underwent a spiritual conversion. Repentant and seeking mercy, he appealed to King James for a second chance. Because the king held his father Arnold in such high regard, Peter was granted a pardon. Responding to the graces offered to him by God, he entered a Mercedarian monastery in Barcelona.

The Mercedarian's mission was to ransom Catholics captured by the Muslims. For eight years, Peter excelled at this task and managed to negotiate the freedom of many hostages from the Saracens. In 1261, he went to Murcia along with William de Bas and freed 213 captives from the Arabs. In 1262 he and Brother Bernard of San Romano went to Granada and freed 202 prisoners. Peter also traveled to Tangiers, Algiers, and Oran, freeing captive Christians in all of those places.

Peter then headed to Africa with Brother William Florentino. His goal was to ransom Christians. On arrival in Bugia, he heard about 18 Christian children held hostage by the Mohammedans. They were under the threat of death if they did not renounce Christianity. Peter offered himself in exchange for the hostages. The captors agreed but warned Peter that he would suffer brutal torture and death if the ransom were not paid on time.

The arrival of the agreed ransom and Friar Peter's release were scheduled for a particular day. The ransom never arrived. Peter was immediately put to torture and endured this for a full day. The Moors, tired of Peter being alive, accused him of blaspheming Mohammad. He was sentenced to be hanged.

The Moors hung Peter Armengol from a tree about a half-mile from the prison walls. His body was left there for the birds of prey to feed on. Six days later, Brother William arrived with the ransom. The Moors refused it and told Friar William that Peter was already dead for six days and his rotted corpse was still hanging from the tree. Distraught, William went to recover his brother Mercedarian's body.

William left and headed to the execution site. As he approached, he noticed that Peter's body seemed to be intact. There was also the fragrance of flowers in the air. William slowly approached the body of Peter. The man who was supposedly dead for six days began to speak. He explained how the Blessed Virgin had come to him and held him up with her precious hands the entire time so his body would not hang on the rope.

When recalling his hanging miracle, Peter Armengol told his Mercedarian brothers that the happiest days of his life were those six days that he hung from the gallows. After all, how could they not be? It was the Blessed Virgin herself, holding him up.

Peter's neck, broken from the hanging, remained in a twisted position for the rest of his life. He always had a sickly complexion and was not pleasant to look at. But Peter Armengol was still happy. The last thing he was concerned about was his appearance. The Blessed Virgin Mary had saved his life. She certainly was not offended by his appearance. Also, seven documented miracles were attributed to him while he was still alive. For Peter Armengol, it was, as they would say eight centuries later, all good.

Peter was 28 years old when he was hung. He lived 38 years after being saved by the Blessed Virgin Mary and died at the age of 66. He was canonized a saint on April 8, 1687, by Pope Innocent XI. He is the patron saint of persecuted Christians.

That story of Peter Armengol is documented history and did happen. Why could it not happen today? The fact is, it could happen. We just need the men and women of faith willing to reach out and accept his challenge. As the cliché goes, maybe "You can do it!"

Fr. Anthony Fortunato O. de M.

Three ladies inspired my vocation to the religious life: Angelina Di Leo in Torchio; my dear mother, Carmela Torchio e Fortunato; and my beloved aunt, Giuseppina Torchio. These ladies took me to church every Sunday and, as a matter of fact, encouraged me to become an altar boy. I also owe a debt of gratitude for the attention and kindness of Pastor Don Antonio Gallo. Father Gallo gave me the first three Sacraments of the Catholic Church in the same Church of the Assumption of Mary, located in Rocca Imperiale, Cosenza, in Calabria.

When I first started to discern my vocation, I wanted to become a diocesan priest. My uncle, Fr. Ferdinando Fortunato, a dear and holy Mercedarian was already stationed and working in our Convitto Villa Mercede in Orvieto, Terni, just north of Rome. During his vacation in August of 1952, he came to Rocca Imperiale. I knew that our Blessed Mother Mary was asking me to go to her Order of Mercy. Adding the call from Our Lady to the example set by Fr. Ferdinando, I knew what I was meant to do. I became a Mercedarian Friar.

So I changed my plans, and instead of going to the minor seminary in Potenza, I went to Nemi, a tiny village near Lake Nemi. It was there that I entered the novitiate for the Mercedarian Friars.

The rest of my story with the Mercedarians has been a great experience. Beginning in Nemi, I then moved to Rome, where I studied at Lateran

University. Then on September 10, 1964, I traveled with three other Mercedarian friars and came to the United States. I lived with the Franciscans for four years while studying theology and education. I was ordained a priest in Frascati, a suburb of Rome, in 1967.

Following my ordination in Frascati, I lived and worked in all the Mercedarian Houses of the Vicariate in the United States. I taught in a high school, worked in our parishes, and served in our formation houses, first in Niagara Falls, New York and later in Philadelphia, Pennsylvania. On August 14, 1984, I came to Florida for the first time. I was stationed at St. Jude's Cathedral. I am now in Florida for the third time, arriving back here in August of 2018.

I am thrilled being a Mercedarian friar and priest. Would I do it all over again? Absolutely! With Jesus and his Mother Mary as my models, I cannot go wrong at all.

I love to be a Mercedarian brother and priest, because I have a cool chance to love Mary of Mercy for the rest of my life in her dear Order. Redemption is the only reason why Jesus came to this world of ours. Saint Peter Nolasco lived for redemption most of his life I will try my very best to be like both of them.

Fr. Tony is the oldest Friar and the last born in Italy. He is in residence at the Peter Nolasco House in St. Petersburg, Florida.

St. Peter Nolasco
Founder of the Mercedarians

T here has been some confusion over the exact birthplace and birth date of Peter. Some historical references say he was born in 1189. However, it is known that he was already redeeming captives in the year 1203. This being the case, he would have required a level of maturity more than someone aged 13 or 14.

Most historians agree that Peter was born either in 1180 or 1182. This makes sense because first, this accounts for the time his Father needed to train him in the art of trading, and second, he would have been a man in his early twenties and more acceptable as a legitimate trader. Dealing and negotiating with the Saracens was no easy task.

The place of birth was Languedoc, located in Toulouse County in Southern France. When Peter was a young boy, the family moved to Barcelona. Once again, there is a touch of controversy. A small number of historians believe that Peter Nolasco was born in a small farmhouse outside Barcelona. But most of the evidence leads to the conclusion that his family had resettled in Barcelona when Peter was a little boy. Most accounts agree that his actual birthplace is Languedoc, Toulouse County, France.

It was said that Peter Nolasco exhibited a compelling and noticeable love for others when he was just a child. A story is told that while Peter was still in his cradle, a swarm of bees stopped in flight and began hovering over him. They circled for a few moments and then landed on his right hand. The bees then proceeded to form a honeycomb and worked until Peter's small hand could not be seen. He was never stung once. People witnessing the event believed that the bees were attracted to the love in the child's heart. This may be true or simply an urban legend. What is certainly true is that Peter Nolasco's interior virtue of love of neighbor was evident to people even when he was just a child.

Peter was a teenager when his father died, probably about fifteen years old. He inherited a substantial amount of money from his father's estate. The young man wanted to be careful with his wealth and prayed for guidance. This was the time in history when the Albigensian heresy was exploding throughout France. Peter, aware of the threat, took his money and headed to Barcelona to be as far away from the Albigensians as possible.

At the same time, the Saracens (Moors) controlled a large part of the Iberian peninsula. They had captured many Christians and put them into bondage. Peter decided that he would begin using his money to ransom Christian prisoners and began ransoming Christian captives in 1203. After fifteen years of helping save captured Christians, he had an in-depth knowledge of the Moors and how to deal with them. He even had several laymen who were his followers. But the money was going fast, and the number of captive Christians was rapidly increasing by the day.

Peter prayed to the Blessed Virgin, asking for her assistance in the rescue of captive Christians. He received Our Lady's answer on August 1, 1218. She appeared to him in a dream and told him that he should transform his lay ministry into a redemptive religious order. By now, the Moors were capturing and enslaving Christians by the thousands. People often heard Peter saying that he would gladly offer himself as ransom if he could. Already experienced at freeing captive Christians, Peter would take the Blessed Virgin's advice and establish a religious order dedicated to helping these victims.

He was already 36 years old and was determined to do as the Blessed Virgin had asked. During the same year of 1218, Raymond of Penafort started a lay organization to ransom slaves. Peter, who was an advocate for this, asked for Penafort's help. He told him he wanted to create an organization made up of religious members under Mary's patronage. Up until this point, the Order was strictly made up of the laity.

Raymond of Penafort encouraged Peter to move forward with his plans. Penafort knew James I, the King of Aragon, and introduced Peter to him. Present at the meeting was the Bishop of Barcelona, Berenguer de Palou. King James and the bishop both liked Peter's idea of starting a redemptive order structured and dedicated to the Blessed Virgin.

On August 10, 1218, the new religious order, called the Religious Order for the Redemption of Captives, was dedicated at the Cathedral of the Holy Cross in Barcelona. They would be known as The Order of the Blessed Virgin Mary of Mercy. The title is summed up in one word: Mercedarians. Bishop Berenguer de Palou gave Peter and his companions the white habit they would wear from that time on. After donning their new habits, they all made their religious vows in the presence of the bishop.

The new Order was solemnly granted approval by Pope Gregory IX in 1230. A special vow bound its members to use all their capabilities for the redemption of captive Christians. In addition to the standard vows of chastity, poverty, and obedience, the Mercedarians would take a fourth vow: they agree to exchange themselves as ransom to free captive Christians. This included their remaining in captivity in place of the captive. In the beginning, most of the members were laymen. However, Pope Clement V decreed that the Master General of the Order always had to be a priest. It followed from then on that others would also study to become priests and reach the heights of ordination.

St. Peter Nolasco never lost sight of the fact that he would join with the Blessed Virgin to advance his ministry. He knew that saving the captives could never be accomplished without help from the Mother of Jesus, and she is linked to the program of liberation and the model for all redemptive work. He knew that Our Lady reinforced and guaranteed all the apostolic works that would be undertaken. She was the foundation of freedom and mercy, the sustenance and point of the liberation movement.

From that point forward, all Mercedarian Friars, Brothers, Sisters, and the Third Order considered Mary the Mother of Freedom. She is the one who sustains and encourages the Order with her ever-continued and ongoing presence. The Blessed Mother came to Peter Nolasco and helped him realize that the mystery of God's redemption is visible in the captivity and heartache of those held against their will.

To this day, Mercedarians will offer themselves by trading their very selves for the freedom of captives. That includes modern-day captivity brought on by society and its secularistic mantra of self-indulgence. The Mercedarians offer help to those who are sick, homeless, or in any way marginalized or oppressed. The Gospel is their guide.

The Mercedarian website states: "Today, friars of the Order of Mercy continue to rescue others from modern types of captivity, such as social, political, and psychological forms. They work in jails, marginal neighborhoods, among addicts, and in hospitals. In the United States, the Order of Mercy gives special emphasis to educational and parish work."

Peter Nolasco died on May 6, 1256. He was canonized a saint by Pope Urban VIII in 1628.

♛ *Feast Day: May 6*

Fr. Matthew Phelan O. de M.

As a child, I loved to put puzzles together, and as I grew older, I began to challenge myself with more challenging puzzles: 500 pieces, 1000 pieces, et cetera. Yet, I could not seem to put the puzzle pieces of my life together. I seemed to struggle with my own identity. It seemed I was a "jack of all trades" and a "master of none."

Although I attended public schools my entire life, I received excellent catechesis through my family and parish. The other kids in CCD would say, "Matthew is going to be a priest." No way! Forget it! Not a chance! My parish priest often suggested that I consider it. Yeah, right! "Thanks, but no thanks, Father." When my mother would bring up the idea of becoming a priest, I would get furious. So, my life went on.

During college, I became lackadaisical in the practice of my Catholicism, just going to Mass when it was convenient or with my parents. I graduated from Marquette University in 1991 with a bachelor of arts in broadcast and electronic communication. I was hired for an entry-level position in a cable company's production department and did some freelance video production. Although I enjoyed my career, something was missing from my life.

I knew that I was lacking in faith and said a simple prayer each night: "Lord, I have no faith, help me." Something inside told me I had to be willing to serve if I were to receive the gift of God's grace. I began to teach the confirmation class at my parish.

Almost immediately after, our whole family went through a transformation. My dad went to a parish mission that profoundly changed him. After speaking with him one weekend, I began to examine my own life. I knew intellectually that the Catholic Church possessed the fullness of faith, but I did not let that truth penetrate my heart.

My initial reaction was the fear of hell. I was well on that path! I returned to the sacrament of penance—it had been about six years—and started attending daily Mass. The fear quickly began to turn into love. My parish had perpetual adoration, and I would stop in to visit Jesus whenever I had a spare moment.

Deep inside, I began to wonder if God had been calling me to the priesthood. Had I been too stubborn to listen to him all these years? Was I merely concerned with what I wanted to do in life? My life was filled with puzzle pieces that did not seem to match. Was I not putting them together correctly? After months of trying to discern whether God was calling me, I sat in the Church reading the scriptures, looking for an answer.

At the height of my frustration, in failing to recognize the answer, I decided it was time for drastic measures—"Bible Roulette." I said to Jesus, "If I am supposed to be a priest, you have to let me know! I can't figure this out! I want to know, *today!* Guide me through your Holy Spirit."

I closed my Bible, closed my eyes, and then opened the Bible and put my finger on the unseen page. Imagine my shock when I opened my eyes, and just above the tip of my finger was Matthew 9:9: "As Jesus passed on from there, he saw a man named Matthew sitting at the customs post. He said to him, 'Follow me.' And he got up and followed him."

I, too, am a man named Matthew, and I have been following Jesus ever since.

Father Matthew Phelan O. De M. is presently the Vicar-Provincial of the U.S. Vicariate and Pastor of Our Lady of Lourdes Parish in Philadelphia, Pennsylvania.

St. Maria de Cervellón

Maria de Cervellón was born in Barcelona on December 1, 1230, and baptized on December 8. in Santa Maria del Mar parish in Barcelona. At that time, the Mercedarian friars had been redeeming captives from the power of the Saracens for several years. Barcelona was a seaport and commercial city. There was talk about the great work of charity undertaken, the growing needs of the friars in financing redemptions, and the upkeep of the Hospital of St. Eulalia, where the ransomed were housed once they returned.

As with every young woman in her time, her family had made other plans for her future. They had tried several times to marry her off to various prominent men to strengthen their familial alliances and position strategically. But one day, she heard a sermon by Bernard de Corbarie, the superior of the Mercedarians. She was so moved by what she heard she vowed right then and there to do all she could to help alleviate the suffering and misery experienced by those who were prisoners of the Muslims.

After that, Maria's heart belonged to another, and she refused each offer her family made on her behalf. She had become the bride of Christ the Redeemer and would spend her life in service to her spouse in the guise of the captive, the wounded, the sick, and the needy. With the assistance of Fr. Bernard, on May 25, 1265, she consecrated herself to God in the Order of Mercy, together with other young women from Barcelona.

Maria was not the first, for there is written evidence that the female branch of the Order of Mercy began earlier. However, she is the first one whose self-offering we know about. From then on her life would be spent between her house and the Hospital of St. Eulalia, located on the shore of Villanova, where it was built thanks to a donation by Raimundo de Plagamans.

The Mercedarian Sisters were not originally formed as a contemplative family, but their life was centered on prayer. They were not founded as cloistered nuns, but gathered in fellowship to live out the Lord's statement: "There is no greater love than to lay down one's life for one's friends." Maria took this call to heart and convinced others to follow the path upon which she had set out. They formed a community of sisters ready to share in the work of redemption, even to the end.

Many believed that Maria had the gift of bilocation. In Spanish, she was known by the surname *de Socós* or *de Socorro* (meaning "helper"), because she was seen coming to the aid of the ransom ships, walking in the midst of the waves of stormy and rough seas, to guide the ships and their precious cargo to safety.

Maria de Cervellón passed away on September 19, 1290. During her life and after her death, some people swore that they saw Maria literally on the "wings of the wind," reaching down and saving floundering ships from rough seas so they might stay their course and continue on their journey to free Christian prisoners from the Muslims.

A great devotion grew in her honor and it was given approval by Pope Innocent XII in 1692. Paintings of Maria de Cervellón show her with a ship cradled in her arms as she saves it from the roaring seas. Her body lies incorrupt to this very day in the Mercedarian Basilica in Barcelona, Spain.

St. Maria de Cervellón is the Patron of Mercedarian Nuns and Sisters, navigators, and the abandoned.

♛ *Feast Day: September 19*

Fr. Pasquale Rosca O. de M.

I entered the religious life in Nemi, Italy in the fall of 1949. Being only 15 at the time, I felt a bit lost; however, there were two religious who came to my rescue: Fr. Rocco Rosca, my uncle, and Fr. Carmine Travisano. Their guidance and encouragement was a great help. They were very simple and strong Mercedarians who always advised obedience to their superiors and dependence on God. These two friars always inspired and guided me in the pains and joys of growing as a young religious. Rightly so, they were there for my profession of vows and for my ordination to the priesthood. They both helped me fulfill my hopes, dreams, and plans.

I was transferred to the United States in 1965 in order to serve at Our Lady of Mount Carmel-West in Cleveland, Ohio. Father Vincent Caruso was there with his simplicity and priestly piety. Following the implementation of the Second Vatican Council in the 1960's, Fr. Vincent was an excellent teacher and model for the religious and the people of God, modeling obedience to the Church and devotion to the Blessed Mother.

In 1976, I was transferred to the Parish of St. Rocco's where I have served to this day. In all of my religious brothers, I experienced the love and witness of Jesus Christ, for the love of Jesus present in the Holy Eucharist, and love of the Blessed Mother. This love enables us to do our best to serve the people.

Fr. Pasquale (Pat) Rosca O. de M. passed away on March 14, 2023, after serving for 74 years as a consecrated religious.

The First Mercedarians in the USA

S aint Peter Nolasco founded the Order in 1218 yet Mercedarian friars did not arrive in the United States until 1915. That is a span of seven centuries. It took 275 years for Mercedarians to make it from Europe to Latin America. Ironically, it was none other than Christopher Columbus who introduced the Mercedarians to the New World. He allowed several of them to travel with him on his second voyage across the Atlantic.

That fleet departed on October 13, 1493, and arrived in Hispaniola sometime near Christmas. Incredibly, it would take another 422 years before the Mercedarians would finally make it to the United States. To put that into perspective, it was still 283 years until the United States was to be born. The four friars who did come were fleeing Mexico for safety reasons.

Plutarco Calles became the Governor of Sonora in Mexico in 1915. Calles was an atheist and hated Catholics, especially priests and religious. To implement his hatred, he managed to use his power to influence having new amendments added to the Mexican Constitution. His hopes were that these articles would turn Mexico into a secular, non-religious country. It would be a country where all religions were prohibited, and priests and other religious, such as nuns and brothers, would be banned.

The Mexican revolution started in 1900 and was still raging in 1915. Calles, who would become president in 1924, instigated violent attacks against religious people, especially foreigners. Among the foreigners were four Mercedarian friars: Martin Compagno, Emil Di Matteo, Raphael Annecchiarico, and James Lassandro.

In the interest of self-preservation, these four men decided to go to the United States and try to establish a community for the Mercedarians. At that time, there were none in the United States. They managed to get letters of credentials from the Master General of the Order, Innocent Lopez Santamaria. The four men left Mexico and arrived in New York City on September 8, 1915.

The four friars were foreigners in a strange land. They spoke little English and had little money. They tried to find Italian neighborhoods where they could communicate with the people. However, the priests needed to secure the local bishop's permission to establish a Mercedarian religious house within his diocese. None of the bishops they spoke to would grant that permission. Instead, the men were offered positions as assistants to the pastors of different parishes. They would have to leave the Mercedarian Order and become diocesan priests subject to the local bishop. Three of the friars agreed and did just that.

Father Martin Compagno chose to remain a Mercedarian friar. He was determined to establish a religious house for the Order in the United States. Father Martin believed the Blessed Virgin would assist him in finding a bishop who would help him get started. Trusting in Mary, he summoned up his patience and began his search. After traveling westward from diocese to diocese, he found himself in a small town in Minnesota called Eveleth. It was April of 1916, and spring was evident as the trees and flowers were once again coming back to life.

Why Fr. Compagno traveled to Minnesota is unknown, but his stay there was short-lived. From Eveleth, he traveled south to Woodbury, Texas. In Woodbury, Fr. Compagno could also use his Spanish to converse with the Mexican laborers and practice his priestly duties. He continued to search for a bishop via letters to different ones in different places.

In 1920 he received an assignment at an Italian parish in Toronto, Canada. He accepted this offer and teamed up with Fr. Raymond Bolados, a Mercedarian from Chile. The two joined forces and began working at St. Agnes parish in Toronto. After a year, Fr. Compagno asked the bishop for permission to establish a Mercedarian community within the diocese. The bishop refused. Father continued to write letters. Among the letters sent was one to the bishop of Detroit, Michigan, and another to the bishop of Cleveland, Ohio. Father Compagno sent these request letters on September 17, 1921. Bishop Joseph Schrembs of Cleveland rapidly sent back his acceptance letter dated October 1, 1921, and a confirmation letter was also received from the diocesan chancellor on October 8. While both bishops sent back letters of acceptance, the more rapid response from Bishop Schrembs was an affirmation of his seriousness, convincing Father this was the right choice.

On October 30, 1921, Fr. Compagno officially took possession of St. Anthony Parish, located in the predominantly Italian section of Youngstown, Ohio. Father Raymond Bolados was assigned as his assistant. After spending five painstaking and arduous years writing different bishops and traveling to various dioceses, Fr. Martin Compagno had finally established the Mercedarian Order in the United States.

The Order took root, and Mercedarian presence began to spread. Today, the Vicariate in the United States has locations in Cleveland, Ohio; LeRoy, New York; Philadelphia, Pennsylvania; St. Petersburg, Florida; and Columbus, Ohio. The friars engage in three primary ministries: parochial service, education, and hospital chaplaincies. These three ministries are also lead-ins for such work as visiting prisons, going to hospice centers to visit and anoint the sick and dying, teaching RCIA candidates, and other pastoral services that fit the charism of the Order.

There are no limitations to what a Mercedarian may be called on to do in service to Jesus. The only problem is there are not enough of these dedicated, Christ-loving children of Our Blessed Lady to feed the ever-increasing demand of starving souls. They are praying that you might consider joining them. All you have to do is pick up the phone or send an email to the vocation office. It is as simple as that, and it may prove to be a life-changing moment for you.

Fr. Eugene Costa O. de M.

One of the most important tasks I can share with you is my vocation story! It has been a special journey to the priesthood and consecrated life in the image of the Mercedarian model.

I'll begin with the first echoes of my vocation. From my earliest recollection, I always wanted to be a priest. Why? To save souls and my own! As a young boy, I loved playing at being a priest, saying the Mass, and doing the benediction. (In fact, I would always be the priest, but my brother had to be the altar boy!) My parents thought it was only a passing phase, but as the years went on, they knew it was my passion.

As a teenager, I went to weekly benediction and was discerning with periodic days of retreat and recollection at the Divine Word Seminary in Duxbury, Massachusetts. Moreover, keeping close to the altar, I was an altar boy. When I graduated high school my hope was to be a priest and that was my goal. But how? I went to my pastor, Msgr. Norton. He told me to apply to the diocesan seminary, the college division being Cardinal O'Connell Seminary in Jamaica Plains, Massachusetts. Monsignor Norton gave me the okay, and a few weeks later, I received word that my application had been accepted. Before I left, my parents told me they were happy only if I was happy. Dad said, "There is no shame if you can't cut it. Remember, you can always come home."

I was happy in the seminary, but little by little, I realized that something was missing. I sensed an unexpected emptiness. I didn't know it then, but the missing piece was community life, something similar to family life. I continued and finished two years in the diocesan seminary before being promoted to the major seminary of St. John's in Boston, Massachusetts. However, I still felt that emptiness that had pervaded me for years.

My journey felt ambivalent, and I had to ask myself tough questions: Where would I go? Should I continue? What is the next step? The months that followed were agonizing, and after much prayer, consultation, and thought, I decided the diocesan priesthood was not for me. My parents thought it was the end of my idea to be a priest. However, to their surprise, I informed them I wanted to become a member of a religious order.

My journey then took another twist: which community should I join? The Holy Spirit was so necessary for my choice, especially in the interviews I made with some communities. I knew they weren't for me. In the archdiocesan newspaper *The Pilot,* I came upon a unique ad for the Mercedarian friars. It was complete with works of mercy. And I wanted to work and be an ambassador of compassion for those enslaved. So I applied with some apprehension. Could this be the community for me?

One of the happiest moments of my vocation story was when I received a phone call from Fr. Esper of the Mercedarians informing me that I was accepted by the Order of Mercy. Instead of a standard letter, he called me. Wow! It was then I found my niche and was truly happy. That emptiness was no longer present, and my newly found community was my home.

My life has had its ups and downs, but I consider it my wonderful joy to be a Mercedarian. What a tremendous love story it is!

Father Eugene Costa is presently a Parochial Vicar at Our Lady of Mercy and St. Bridgid Parish in Leroy, New York

Our Lady of Bonaria and the Miracle of the Chest Lost at Sea

T his is the story of the Patroness of Sardinia, also known as Our Lady of Bonaria. It is one of those remarkable stories that are part of Mercedarian history. What follows took place 650 years ago. Incredibly, Mercedarians have been serving on this site since 1335.

Carlo Catalano was a Mercedarian friar who founded the Mercedarian convent in Cagliari, Italy. The year was 1324, and Brother Carlo had a dream. He dreamt that a statue of Santa Maria de Bonaria would be arriving there. He and his brother Mercedarians were ready to receive it. Brother Carlo insisted they had to be prepared for her arrival every day since they did not know when she would come. And so the wait began.

Tradition says that on the Feast of the Annunciation, March 25, 1370, a ship traveling from Spain to Italy sailed into a terrible storm off the coast of Sardinia. The sailors were sure the boat would sink, so they began throwing cargo over the sides to lighten the load.

The last crate was unbelievably heavy, and the sailors could barely lift it. As soon as they managed to get it over the side and it hit the water, the storm stopped, the winds subsided, and the sea turned calm. They tried desperately to retrieve the crate, but it disappeared. Days later, unknown to the sailors, the chest washed up on Sardinia's shore at the foot of a hill called Bonaria.

There was a large crowd of people on the beach when the big wooden box floated onto the shore. They all hurried to see what it might be. Try as they may, they could not open nor move it; it was too heavy. A child in the crowd cried out, "Call the Mercedarians. They will be able to open it."

The nearby church and monastery had been under the care of the Mercedarians since 1335. The people hurried to the church and asked the friars to come with them to see the mysterious chest. When the friars arrived at the beach, they could lift the box without effort.

A large crowd followed the friars carrying the box to the church. They were able to open it up without a bit of trouble. Inside the box, they found something that amazed everyone there. It was a statue of Our Blessed Mother holding the Christ Child. In the Virgin's left hand was a candle. The candle was lit.

Unknown to those present, they had just witnessed the fulfillment of a prophecy. When the church was built in 1330, Fr. Carlo Catalano was the ambassador to the Aragonese Court. During the dedication, he told the monks, "A Great Lady will come to live in this place. After her coming, the malaria infecting this area will disappear, and her image will be called the Virgin of Bonaria."

The friars, recalling the priest's words, named the statue "Our Lady of Good Air." They called it this because of the winds that had blown the sculpture across the sea to Bonaria. Due to the miracle, word spread quickly among the people.

To this day, sailors invoke the Blessed Virgin as their protectress. The devotion is still honored and practiced in many places around the world. In 1536, the founder of Argentina, Pedro de Mendoza, named the country's capital after Our Lady of Bonaria, calling it, "Buenos Aires," literally "Holy Mary of the Fair Winds."

In 2008, Pope Benedict XVI, on the Feast of Mary's Nativity, visited the shrine. He gave a canonical coronation to the famous statue. Pope Francis made a repeat apostolic visit to Sardinia in September 2013.

The Mercedarians have staffed and continually cared for the Shrine of Our Lady of Bonaria for over 680 years. Brother Carlo and his brother Mercedarians waited patiently for 35 years, never doubting the Virgin's arrival. Mercedarians are at this shrine to this day, standing watch the same as their ancestors from centuries ago.

Ms. Anne DeSantis

Director of the Raymond Nonnatus Foundation

My name is Anne DeSantis. I live in the Philadelphia area, and I am a Third Order member of the Mercedarian Religious Order. I became a consecrated member of the Third Order of Mercy in 2017, joining my husband, Angelo. I love the Mercedarian charism, especially the fourth vow, which is "the willingness to offer our lives for those in danger of losing their faith."

In 2009, our daughter—who was grade school age—was presented with challenges that affected all of us. Our family pulled together to help her through emotional challenges that thankfully have been resolved, and we are grateful.

With this being said, I prayed more than ever and had started to look for a new spiritual director. I had found a good one, but unfortunately, it was a priest who had cancer, and within the year, he died. Shortly after, I found a good religious sister who became my spiritual director. The same thing happened, and she passed away from cancer. This all occurred during 2012. It was four years after my daughter's issues, and I was still recovering from the difficult period of watching my child suffer.

After the second spiritual director died, I wanted to find a new one, but I had an exceedingly difficult time. I called my archdiocese and I asked friends, but no one seemed to have a good referral for me. Finally, I started to call around at churches hoping to find a priest or religious. After a long time searching, I looked in a book called *The Catholic Directory* and I found The Monastery of Our Lady of Mercy. I did not know what this was, so I called the number.

Brother Daniel Bowen picked up the phone. He was genuinely nice to me, and I told him my story. He took the time to listen and to care. I told him I might need a spiritual director. He said he had not been ordained yet, but that Fr. Matthew Phelan, who also lived at the Monastery, would be a good one for me if he could.

I talked to Fr. Matthew, and he became my spiritual director for a few years. I got to know all the Mercedarians in the community. Father Matthew not only got to know me, he also got to know my family! He even came over with several of the friars for dinner at our house and became one of the family along with some of the other religious. It was so comforting to have the support and outreach after having gone through such difficult times.

In 2015, the friars in Philadelphia decided to start a non-profit called "The St. Raymond Nonnatus Foundation for Freedom, Family, and Faith." An event was scheduled with little help to organize it from within the Foundation. Father Matthew asked me if I would be willing to help out as administrative assistant. My duties would be to assist with the event and to work in the Foundation. My answer was, "Yes!"

I was promoted to director in January 2018. Our mission is to provide spiritual accompaniment to families in crisis and Catholics affected by divorce. It has been my honor to serve in that capacity to the present time.

We offer spiritual consultation with a Mercedarian friar as a free service. We produce podcasts, online shows, and of course, most importantly, we offer prayer. We also provide helpful resources on our website at *Nonnatus.org*. Father Ken Breen O. de M. serves as our Spiritual Moderator. His job is to talk to our clients about the issues they have regarding being a family in crisis and those affected by divorce, including the adult children of divorce.

There are countless stories of how we have helped people in the Foundation. Many people find out about us through the internet and through referrals. They come to us seeking healing. Since one of our primary offerings is free spiritual consultation, Fr. Ken will offer as many sessions as needed to our clients, to listen and pray for them. We have people who have come away from abusive relationships wishing to find healing and reconciliation with a spouse. We always pray for healing even if some of the relationships will be severed, and the annulment process will begin. These people come to us looking for someone who will care, listen, and offer support. We also provide help for marriages to be enriched in many ways, and we have excellent resources.

Some of our clients have become active volunteers, and they have been guests on our podcasts. This brings about great healing as many of them are healed by helping other people. One woman has been a guest on our podcast several times, and she has even brought in several friends to learn more about our mission. We are grateful to all of those who have trusted us.

Father Ken and some of the friars have been wonderful in making outreach to our clients in crisis. You can subscribe to our YouTube channel at "Philly Nonnatus" or visit our website *Nonnautus.org* to find out more. The St. Raymond Nonnatus Foundation is fulfilling the mission of helping families in crisis.

My story is just one in the wonderful Mercedarian Order. We also have a fourth vow which is our willingness to give our lives to those in danger of losing their faith. I am a professed member of the Third Order of Mercy and finalized my promises to the Order in 2017. We hold each other in prayer. It is wonderful to get to know people from all over the country professing themselves and living as a Third Order Mercedarian. Most of all, it is a true blessing that my husband is also a Third Order member of the online group. The Third Order is truly a blessing in my life.

Fr. Juan Gilberto–Jofre and Our Lady of the Forsaken

On Friday, February 24, 1409, Fr. Juan Gilberto-Jofre, a Mercedarian priest, was walking to the cathedral to say Mass. He heard a commotion in the street and saw a man on the ground covering his head with his arms as a gang of young people were taunting, mocking, and hitting him.

Father Jofre hurried over to the small crowd and demanded they stop hurting one of God's children. Father Jofre rescued the man and brought him to the Mercedarian monastery, where he was given shelter and had his wounds tended to. He also realized the young man was mentally challenged. The following Sunday at Mass, he preached his first sermon about the mentally ill.

In the sermon, he included a plea for funds to build a place to care for and shelter these people. He was so forceful in his speech that the merchants, artisans, and business people at the Mass gave generously. The money became available, and before long a home and hospital opened dedicated to the Blessed Mother under the title of "Our Lady of Innocents."

On August 29, 1414, a brotherhood was founded dedicated to caring for the mentally ill. It was called the Brotherhood of Our Lady of the Insane and the Forsaken Innocents. That name would soon change. A famine had struck the land, and many children had been orphaned. The Brotherhood quickly extended its care to the mentally ill and the many orphaned children wandering the streets of Valencia. The name was changed, and the new dedication was to Our Lady of the Forsaken.

Father Jofre and his brother friars realized the hospital lacked a prayer room. They built an oratory and, when they finished, knew it was missing something: a statue of Our Lady of the Forsaken. Since there was no such statue, they prayed for help in acquiring one.

Legend has it that soon after, three handsome young men knocked on the door seeking refuge. They offered to carve the needed statue as payment for allowing them to stay. They only asked to be left alone to work for at least three days. The friars accepted the offer.

The three young men remained locked inside the room as the three days passed. The friars would listen by the door, but no sound was heard. At the end of the third day, they knocked on the door again, but there was still no answer. Finally, they forced open the door only to find the three men gone. They found a magnificent statue that the men had created, sitting in the center of the room.

Who were these handsome men? Their identity was never discovered, but most folks quickly came to believe they were angels sent by God. Miracles began to happen, starting with the wife of a member of the Brotherhood. Paralyzed and blind, she was completely cured. Thus began the legend called *"Elferen els angels,"* or "Made by the Angels."

The statue exhibited a demeanor that was called "majestic and protective." The people took this to mean that it signified the goodness, mercy, and assistance which comes from someone majestic. In 1885 the statue was named the *"Virgen de Los Desamparados"* or "Our Lady of the Forsaken" and declared the Patroness of Valencia.

The hospital that Fr. Juan Gilberto-Jorfe founded became the very first mental hospital in the world. It was dedicated to the Blessed Mother under the title of "Our Lady of Innocents." For the first time anywhere, there was a place to provide care and medical attention to the mentally ill while at the same time sheltering them. Today it is called the University Teaching Hospital of the University of Valencia.

Father Jofre died on May 18, 1417, and is buried at the Monastery of El Puig. The cause for Fr. Jofre's canonization was stalled twice in the early eighteenth century during the Napoleonic Wars. Documentation was also destroyed during the Spanish Civil War of 1936. The process has finally been revived, and Fr. Jofre was declared a Servant of God in 2007. His cause for canonization has been referred to the Holy See in Rome.

Today there is a Basilica of Our Lady of the Forsaken in Valencia, where the statue is displayed. Every year on the second Sunday of May, a huge festival is held in honor of Our Lady of the Forsaken Ones. It is said that St. Bonaventure is quoted as saying, "When all human help fails, it is imperative that we not despair. For normally in this extreme situation, the divine help of Mary comes," thus connecting him to Our Lady of the Forsaken.

Fr. Kenneth Breen O. de M.

I was born in Rumson, New Jersey, and raised in Westlake, Ohio, a suburb of Cleveland. I was the second of nine children born over ten years, and our home was a boisterous and active place. I remember lots of laughter and fun vacations and camping trips, but most of all, we were a solid Catholic family. We lived within the parish boundaries of St. Richard's, and I attended school there from first through eighth grade.

I had an ongoing anxiety problem that amped itself up toward the end of each school year. I was always afraid of not being promoted to the next grade. When I received my final report card for the year, I opened it ever so slowly, praying I had made it to the next grade. I always did. I would carry that fear throughout my educational history.

Thinking I could escape this anxiety by attending the diocesan high school seminary across town, I applied and was accepted there. I figured all the students would be strangers to me and would ignore me. The thought of becoming a priest was not a factor in my going to a preparatory school for the priesthood. My true motive was to escape the cycle of torment.

My high school experience proved worse than it was in grade school. The students there seemed to all know each other, and I was an outsider. I was taunted and felt alone. I did make friends with several guys, and one would become my best friend. His name was Mike Diemer, and he would prove to be a significant influence in my life.

I graduated high school and opted out of attending the diocesan college seminary. I had learned that the life of a diocesan priest was much more isolated than the orders of priests who live in a community. I did not want to be alone, so I pushed my religious vocation to the side. I decided to follow my sister and enroll in Cleveland State University. I considered majoring in accounting, but my true love was science and math, so I chose chemical engineering as a major.

During my first year at Cleveland State, I was happy enough. I was accepted into my sister's circle of friends, which included guys and gals. However, in our second year, that group had become almost non-existent as members moved in different directions. I missed belonging to a circle of friends, and I realized I also needed love.

In the summer of 1977, my best friend from high school, Mike Diemer, came to visit me. I was thrilled to see Mike, and we talked and reminisced all day and into the night. As the day progressed, this visit began to turn into one of the most meaningful experiences of my young life. Mike, who was attending the diocesan college seminary in Cleveland, began sharing the richness of the Catholic faith with me.

He taught me the reality of Jesus truly present in the Most Holy Eucharist. He deepened that reality by going over the Fatima story with me. He explained how the children were called to reverence Jesus truly present in the Most Holy Eucharist and how they were shown a vision of Hell. They learned that many sinners go there because they have no one to pray for them.

Then Mike instilled in me an understanding of the reality of God as existence itself. He showed me how God is the Great I Am, the only reality whose very nature is to exist. Mike explained how in Jesus, he continues his authority to teach and guide us through the successors of Peter in the Magisterium of the Catholic Church. Understanding this gave me great confidence in the presence and power of God in Jesus. It brought about a profoundly healing conversion experience filled with such joy that it remains with me to this day. But that does not mean that life has been a piece of cake.

Challenges to grow in virtue never end, and struggles were always there for me, like almost everyone. By my second year in college, I did not see any development that might lead to married life. I was willing, but the girls I was attracted to had other interests, and they never included me. Maybe it was my fault in how I approached girls or talked to them. I do not know. I do know that I turned to Jesus and asked him to show me the path to follow.

One thing I knew for sure: I did not want to live life alone. I prayed about this every day. Crises in my family over prayer were something emotionally supercharged. Mom wanted to pray the Rosary, but others did not want to bother. I made a commitment to be there with my parents for the family Rosary, even though my siblings were not. Our Lady of Fatima called for praying the Rosary, and I was determined to be with my Mom. I began attending daily Mass whenever I could, from which I received great joy.

I was only a college kid but for me going to Mass was out of this world. Unexpectedly, my attendance at daily Mass would ultimately lead me to the Mercedarians. God has such subtle, albeit powerful, ways of signaling us about what he wants us to do. He messaged me with a sign in the church narthex as I was leaving Mass.

As I walked toward the church exit, I noticed a poster with a Saturn V rocket on it. It showed a young boy looking out a window staring at this incredible rocket lifting off from the launch pad. The caption emblazoned across the poster said, "No Greater Love." I did have a great interest in science, but I was also looking for love combined with science. And here it was, a proposal just for that. I grabbed the postcard from the poster, filled it out, and mailed it in. By the end of the day, I think it had passed from my mind.

I began the New Year of 1978 sort of stuck without anything prompting me to my life choices. Married life seemed to evade me continually, but I did not give up and kept asking our Lord to show me the way. As the Lenten season began, I embraced the St. Louis de Montfort Consecration to the Immaculate Heart of Mary. Not long after, I was at a Sunday evening Mass. The Gospel was about the Apostles fishing all night and catching nothing. As dawn was breaking, they heard a voice calling out, asking if they had caught anything. They yelled back, "Nothing!"

Then they heard these words, "Throw the net over the other side of the boat."

Some of them laughed at such a ridiculous suggestion, but Peter did not. He told his friends to do what the voice said. They grudgingly pulled the heavy net out of the water and tossed it over the other side. Within minutes the net is filled, and they have a huge catch. They immediately knew it was Jesus. He not only brought them a great catch, he also brought them a healing peace. This also came with a perk: a great breakfast.

He called again, "Come follow me." That suddenly made me remember the card I had mailed in. I realized I had never even checked to see if there was a response. It dawned on me I had better check the counter when I got home.

When I got home, I went right to the counter, and sure enough, there was an envelope addressed to me mixed with other mail. It was from the Mercedarians, and I had no idea how long it had been there. I quickly took it to my room and sat down at my small desk. Over it hung a picture of Jesus and on it was a small statue of Our Lady of Grace. I enjoyed having them there with me, and I would pray in front of them.

I held the envelope and looked at it for a few moments. God is amazing because I knew that inside this envelope was the answer to my future life. I opened the envelope and before anything else happened a message came to me. It said, "Come follow me."

Longing and wondering about love, this was the moment that introduced me to our Order. Later on, another sign that only our Lord could arrange led me to have the confidence to begin a journey that I trusted then and I still trust now. That is to live out "no greater love in his wonderful hands." I have never doubted that moment. I threw my net from science and engineering into the Mercedarian life, which included the priesthood, and I never looked back.

He who made us truly knows the plan for our eternal joy. Trusting that he is Lord just as Abraham did and journeyed to joy in the Promised Land, and the Apostles trusted to throw the net on the other side of the boat for that unbelievable catch, so I launched into that trust to give my life to "no greater love." I pray for the grace to live it fully everyday.

Father Ken has been a priest of the Order of the Blessed Virgin Mary of Mercy for over 35 years. He has held a number of positions and ministries, including serving as novice master for the Roman Province's mission in India for many years; a prison chaplain in St. Petersburg, Florida; parochial vicar at St. Rocco and Our Lady of Mount Carmel-West in Cleveland, Ohio; and Vicar-Provincial for the United States Vicariate. Father Ken Breen is presently the Superior at the Peter Nolasco House in St. Petersburg, Florida.

Blessed Mariana of Jesus Navarro

On January 17, 1565, a baby girl was born to Ludovico Navarro Guevara and his wife, Joan Romero. She was the first of six children, and the only girl born into the family. The child was baptized four days after her birth and given the name Mariana. When her mom passed away, Mariana was still a youngster. Her dad was like a small boat adrift without his wife being there. His young daughter became his mooring as he leaned on her for help with his sons. But she was very young, and although she tried her best to keep her dad happy, it was a bit overwhelming for her. Being expected to become a replacement "mother" to her younger brothers was a role she could not fill. Her father knew it.

After a short time, Mariana's dad remarried. The pressure of caring for her brothers was minimized. However, Mariana's stepmother did not like her new stepdaughter very much and treated her coldly and aloofly. The youngster could feel the woman's indifference, but she could do nothing about it.

Mariana's father wanted his daughter to get married so she would leave home. He assumed that her leaving would help reduce the ongoing tension that filled the house. But Mariana did not want to get married. She wanted to serve Jesus and live in prayer and service to others.

Mariana had grown into a beautiful young woman and was pious and spiritual. When her parents told her they had found a suitable suitor, Mariana told them of her wish to serve God and become a nun. She did not want to marry anyone but Jesus Christ and devote her life to him. She was already 23 and turned down the proposal.

Mariana's parents were furious at her. They tried to keep her at home and make her life miserable. She fought back by cutting off her long hair to make herself less attractive. She became a virtual prisoner in her own home. This unhappy existence was Mariana's plight for the foreseeable future. Ten years later, her father relented and allowed her to leave home to answer her calling to Christ. Soon after leaving home, she met Fr. John Baptist of the Blessed Sacrament, a Mercedarian priest. He was the person who would provide her with the needed spiritual direction she had been seeking.

At last, free to concentrate on her search for the sanctity she desired, she began her journey. Mariana had taken ill several years before and was in a permanently weakened state. Her condition prevented her from entering a convent and living the demanding, disciplined life required to be part of the community. With Fr. John Baptist's help, she managed to find a small cottage near the convent close to the Mercedarian Church in Madrid. She was able to pay the small rent because her well-to-do father had given her a stipend to live on.

Mariana entered into a life of daily prayer and devotion. Under the guidance of Fr. John and with his recommendation, Mariana professed private vows of chastity and obedience as a Mercedarian Tertiary, taking the religious name of Sister Mariana of Jesus. Finally, in 1614, at the age of 49, she professed her final vows and spent the rest of her life serving the sick and the poor.

After becoming a consecrated layperson, Sister Mariana's spiritual life continued to grow as she committed to voluntary daily penance, social work, and especially spending hours before Christ present in the Blessed

Sacrament. Sister Mariana spent as much time as possible kneeling in front of the tabernacle. She would be fully absorbed in Christ before her, and nothing could distract her. Sister Mariana began exhibiting mystical gifts, including levitations, healing power, and soul discernment. Many people started coming to her, and she used her gifts to counsel and pray with them.

Mariana Navarro de Jesus died on April 17, 1624, in Madrid. People from many different places came to pay their respects. Huge crowds formed to honor and venerate the holy lady they called the "Lily of Madrid." The smell of fresh flowers was said to have filled the air near Mariana's remains. Miracles were reported during her lifetime and continued after her passing.

Sister Mariana's body was exhumed in 1627, 1731, 1765, and again in 1924. Each time her body was incorrupt. Only God can make such inexplicable things happen. Today, people still come from all over the world to witness the incorrupt body of this saintly woman. In 2024 it will be 400 years since her passing. Pilgrims will still be coming and marveling at one of God's special people.

Pope Pius VI beatified Sister Mariana Navarro de Jesus on May 25, 1783.

♛ *Feast Day: April 27*

Fr. Michael Donovan O. de M.

My name is Michael Joseph Donovan, and I am a religious friar of the Order of the Blessed Virgin Mary for the Redemption of Christian Captives. We are also known as the Order of the Blessed Virgin Mary of Mercy and, for the most part, are referred to as Mercedarians.

As with most people called to religious life, my journey was rather complicated and took many turns. I grew up in a large family and was the youngest of four sisters and two brothers. My dad was a non-practicing Roman Catholic, and my mom was a practicing Presbyterian and she made me attend Bible study in the Presbyterian church.

I was seven years younger than my closest sister, and as my circle of friends developed, I became exposed to the Catholic faith for the first time. They invited me to attend their church. I already felt a strong attraction to that religion, and I was happy to accept the invitation.

I remember as if it were yesterday the first time I went to a Catholic church and attended the Holy Sacrifice of the Mass. The church's beauty affected me deeply, and when I came to understand that the Holy Eucharist was the Real Presence of Jesus, I immediately knew I had to become Catholic. I was only eleven years old when I asked my mom and dad if I could have their permission to become Catholic. By a special grace from God, they said "yes."

Following my entrance into the Catholic faith, I asked my parents if I could attend Catholic school; to this request, they also agreed. I began attending St. Robert Bellarmine Catholic School in Chester, Pennsylvania. At St. Robert's, the beauty of Catholicism was presented to me in a powerful way. God had brought me into a world with outstanding priests, sisters, and laypeople. Inspired by the faith, prayer, and love I witnessed in the priests and sisters at St. Robert's, I realized I wanted to be like them and follow in their footsteps.

I attended St. James Catholic High School for boys, also in Chester. During my high school years, I worked during the evenings at the church rectory, answering the phone and greeting visitors. Throughout my four years in high school my attraction to religious life continued to grow. My sophomore year proved to be very special. I had the honor and privilege to travel on a pilgrimage to Fatima, Portugal, and visit the site where the Blessed Virgin appeared to the three shepherd children in 1917. It was at this time I placed my future in Our Lady's hands. I would need her help more than I could imagine as a true challenge awaited me. As I entered my senior year in high school, I was confident that religious life was in my future.

Toward the end of my senior year, something disastrous and shocking occurred in my life: I failed both trigonometry and physics, and I was not allowed to graduate with my class. I not only failed both of those subjects, I felt like I had personally failed myself. I believed that God would not call me now, so I gave up on pursuing a religious vocation. What I had actually done was say "no" to God, and I continued to say "no" to God for the next eight years.

I decided to become a high school Spanish teacher. I moved on and attended college, receiving a degree in Spanish. At the same time, I had a great accounting job. But I knew in my heart I was not doing what God willed for me. This truth made me quite unhappy. It was time for me to listen to that truth.

When I started in earnest to heed God's call things began moving forward rather easily. I remember my first visit to a Mercedarian community. I was immediately attracted to the communal life of brotherhood and prayer and the living out of the evangelical counsels of poverty, chastity, and obedience. Any doubts I had were gone, and I immediately felt at home. I knew right then and there that God was calling me to religious life.

As I came to learn about the unique charism of the Mercedarian Order, I fell in love with it. The Mercedarian charism is so beautifully unique because it is, in all actuality, a three-fold charism of redemption, divine worship, and Marian devotion. God sure does draw us to himself in unexpected ways. I have only one regret: that it took me so long to trust him.

I am still learning to trust. Perhaps not trusting in God's love, mercy and Divine Providence has been my greatest weakness. Each brand new day he gives me evidence to trust him.

Father Donovan is presently Superior and Pastor at Holy Family parish and the Mercedarian House of Studies in Columbus, Ohio. His motto at this stage of his life is, "Through Mary, He must increase, and I must decrease."

Brother Matthew Levis O. de M.

I t all started at the age of 16 when my grandmother said that when I was eight years old I told her that I was going to be a priest. At 16 years of age, I had no desire to be a priest, and I laughed at my grandmother. It was my intention to get a girl, go out on some dates and eventually get married.

Within a few years I started to take more interest in church-related activities. I had always been an altar boy and sang in the choir regularly. I soon began to lector, and when needed, I ushered at Mass. Eventually, I even became a religious education teacher. Even though I participated in all of these activities, I never thought much of entering religious life. Mom and dad always encouraged the priestly life, as did my uncle, a priest, but I still did not hear God's call for me.

When I was in ninth grade, my religion teacher, a nun, constantly nagged me about being a priest. She told me to look into it and that I had a vocation. To get her off my back, of course, I told her I would. That solved the problem for a week. Afterward, she asked if I did look into it, and I could not lie to the good sister, so I said no. Then she started nagging me again. Not long after that, my pastor came to me and handed me an envelope. He said to call the number inside and talk to them. So I figured I better do it because this time, it was the priest who told me to do it.

As I began to foster my vocation, I was a little uncomfortable because I did not want to be a priest. But I still wanted to live in a community. My mother suggested looking into the brotherhood. When I looked into the community my pastor suggested, I realized a whole new world was waiting for me to explore. It was a matter of finding out which community best fit me.

After looking into three to four different communities and entering two of them, I determined that they were not the right communities for me. My age was working against me, so I decided that I would try one more time, and if this did not work, I would approach my local bishop and ask to take private vows.

How I found this community is quite simple. I opened up the *Catholic Digest* to the back where all the ads are for religious life, and pointed to the most prominent ad on the page. I never read the ad. I just called to learn more about them, only to realize that it was a perfect fit. This order is The Order of Our Lady of Mercy.

When I was accepted into the Mercedarians, I called my grandmother to share with her the good news. When I told her, the first thing I heard was her laugh.

Brother Matthew presently is assigned to St. Rocco's Parish in Cleveland, Ohio

A Mercedarian Walks Into a Diner

We Catholics hear much about evangelizing and evangelization. The first major papal document by Pope Francis was the apostolic exhortation *Evangelii Gaudium* or "The Joy of the Gospel." I believe evangelizing starts with each one of us. We just have to be willing to say the name of Jesus in public. I am not suggesting that we stand on a street corner screaming his name. Instead, when we are with others, friends, relatives, and even people online or at the supermarket, we should wait for the opportunity to present itself where we can mention Jesus' name. What is the "right opportunity?" It is all about sensing the moment. This is not science. You have to "feel it" and take a chance. You may be rejected. And you may not be, which is most of the time. What follows is from personal experience. It is one of my evangelizing favorites.

I carry small wooden crosses in my pocket. They are called pocket crosses or comfort crosses. They are small enough to wrap your hand around. Recently, a spontaneous and evangelizing moment presented itself at a local family restaurant in the town in which I live. The town's name is Pinellas Park, located on the Florida west coast. The diner is aptly called the Parkside Café. My friends and I go there often.

A short while ago, they hired a new busboy. I began talking to him, and I found out his name was Brian. He was a junior at Dixie Hollins High School, which was nearby. After about two weeks, I saw him again, and we began to talk. I had a feeling, so I asked him, "Hey Brian, do you love Jesus?"

He replied, "Yes, I do." So I pulled a comfort cross from my pocket and handed it to him. Our eyes were locked as I explained how he could carry it in his pocket, and he always would have a friend named Jesus nearby who he could hold onto if needed.

A few weeks later, Fr. Daniel Bowen O. de M. was visiting from Cleveland. We saw him on Friday, and he was supposed to leave Saturday morning, but his flight was put off until six-o'clock that evening.

Several of us were at Parkside Saturday morning for breakfast. Brian was working, and he was filling my coffee cup. In comes Fr. Daniel. I wave him over, and I quickly tell him about Brian. Then I asked Brian if he would mind if Father blessed him. He agreed. The Mercedarians wear white habits with a large, white scapular over the back and front. They also wear their distinctive black *Saturnos* hats.

Parkside was packed. Standing next to our table in the middle of the dining room, Fr. Daniel began an unplanned, spontaneous, and powerful evangelization moment at the Parkside Café.

Father raised his hands over Brian's bowed head. All heads turned to watch this Catholic moment. Father prayed for maybe two minutes. Then he blessed Brian. It was no quick blessing as Fr. Daniel's hand made a large sign of the cross vertically from above Brian's head down to his waist and then up and horizontally from shoulder to shoulder. It was a marvelous visual for the hundred or more patrons who quietly watched. Talk about a spontaneous evangelization moment. It was awesome. I heard later from one of the servers that the whole place was abuzz about the priest and the blessing.

Interestingly, it all started with one pocket cross given to one teenager. That morphed into over a hundred people witnessing a Catholic priest bless and lay hands on that teenager. I have no idea if any of those folks witnessing those moments were brought to Jesus. But I know they were all thinking about him.

St. Peter Paschal

P eter Paschal was born in Valencia on Spain's east coast in the year 1227. Peter's parents were devout *Mozarabs* (Iberian Christians) who managed to live under Muslim rule. They did this by paying a yearly tax, known as *jizyah*. This tax was collected to spare the life of certain non-Muslims living in the community. It all depended upon whether or not the ruling Imam decided a particular person deserved death. The Mozarabs and the Muslim Arabs co-existed and even spoke a common language known as *Mozarabic*.

The founder of the Mercedarians, St. Peter Nolasco, was close friends with the Paschal family. He and his Mercedarian companions would often stay at the Paschal home when they were on a mission to free Christian captives. Exposure to these pious men helped to instill in young Peter Paschal a robust faith. Combined with his parents' virtuous, charitable, and caring influence, Peter Paschal grew into a deeply devoted servant of God.

Ironically, the primary influence in Peter's educational journey was a teacher that his parents had ransomed from the Muslim Moors years before. The young Peter traveled with him to Paris and, under his guidance, Peter studied, preached, and taught, developing a fine reputation as a learned and pious man.

Peter Paschal then returned to Valencia, and Peter Nolasco became his spiritual advisor. After another year of preparation, he became a full member of the Mercedarians. It was time for him to begin redeeming captive Christians.

Peter Paschal had a brilliant mind, and James I, the King of Aragon, appointed him as a teacher of his son, Sanchez. Peter so influenced the king's son that in 1262, Sanchez became a Mercedarian priest. Prince Sanchez was named the Archbishop of Toledo, but since he was too young to receive consecration as bishop, his teacher, Peter Paschal, was appointed to govern the diocese as titular bishop. Peter was thus consecrated as the Bishop of Granada, which was under the control of the Muslims.

As Bishop of Grenada, Peter Paschal, preached tirelessly about Christianity. He became known for his intense determination and zeal to redeem captive enslaved Christians imprisoned by the Moors. His preaching was so potent that many Muslims began to embrace the doctrines of Jesus Christ and convert to Christianity. The followers of Mohammad began to harbor intense and growing anger toward Peter.

Besides preaching, Peter not only continually ransomed captive Christians from the Moors, but he also comforted those imprisoned and preached the gospel to the infidels. His ability to reconcile apostates and others and bring them to the church was the reason he was finally arrested and placed in a dark dungeon. The jailers were given orders that no one was allowed to speak to Peter Paschal.

Peter was held in prison and constantly treated cruelly. But, strange as it may seem, he was permitted to offer the Holy Sacrifice of the Mass every day. And this is where the wonderful legend of St. Peter Paschal springs to life.

One morning, while preparing for Mass, Peter realized he had no altar server. He usually could have one of the prisoners he had converted serve for him, but this day he could find no one to serve. Suddenly, a little boy about the age of five appeared before the priest. The boy was dressed in the clothes of a slave and asked Peter what he was looking for. Peter told him he needed an altar server.

The boy told Bishop Peter he would gladly serve Mass for him if Peter would let him. Peter asked the boy who he was, and the boy said, "I will tell you who I am when you have finished Mass."

After Mass was finished, Peter asked the boy a few questions and was amazed at the wisdom coming forth from the child. Then he asked the boy, "Tell me, who is Jesus Christ?"

The boy answered: "I am Jesus Christ; it is I who was crucified for your salvation and for that of the whole world. Look at my hands, and my feet, and my side, and you will recognize the wounds I received during my passion. Because you have of your own choice remained a prisoner to procure freedom for my captive children, and because to obtain their freedom you spent money sent to procure your own, you have made me your prisoner."

As mysteriously as he had appeared, the little boy disappeared. Peter Paschal was filled with an indescribable joy. He knew that Jesus, as a little boy, had been his altar server.

The Muslims sensed and actually revered the sanctity of their prisoner. They told Peter if he would never say anything against Mohammad, they would give him his freedom. He said he could never make such a promise. Shortly thereafter, as Bishop Peter Paschal said his thanksgiving after Mass, a Muslim executioner came up from behind him and cut off his head. The date was January 6, 1300.

Bishop Peter Paschal was beatified and canonized by Pope Clement X on August 14, 1670.

👑 *Feast Day: December 6*

Fr. David Spencer O. de M.

My parents had me begin my schooling by attending private school. The school I attended only taught up to fourth grade so, towards the end of third grade, they began looking for a different private school for me. Mom and dad were determined that I receive a quality education. After a purposeful search, they found Christ the King Catholic School right in our hometown of Norfolk, Virginia. They enrolled me there, and I would stay in this school until eighth grade. The irony was, we were not Catholic. I would be one of only three non-Catholics in my class.

It was quite different for me culturally. Our days in school always began with prayer. But before we prayed, we always had to bless ourselves by making the Sign of the Cross. We also blessed ourselves when we finished praying. We had daily Catechism classes, attended Mass every day, and had frequent visits by Fr. Joseph Layman, the pastor of Christ the King. The other two non-Catholic students and I were not permitted to receive Holy Communion. We had to remain in the pew, kneeling, while the other kids all received. I felt left out, and it made me feel as if I was not part of my class. I did not like the feeling. After finishing fourth grade, I asked my parents if I could become Catholic

Mom and dad were not Catholic and did not understand Catholicism. Their concern focused on the quality of my education, and they were pleased with how that part of my young life was progressing. But my mom understood me and realized why I had requested to become Catholic. She went to see the school principal, Mrs. Sarocki. She referred my mom to Fr. Layman.

Father Layman was a kind man and he sat my mother down and explained the entire process of becoming Catholic to her. I began intense Catechism study, attended RCIA (Rite of Christian Initiation) and during the Easter Vigil of 1994, I was accepted into the Catholic Church. I was eleven years old. The truth was, I believe I became Catholic because I "wanted that little white thing"—Christ present in the consecrated Host—so I could receive communion with my other classmates. But even though I wanted to be like the other kids, my conversion to Catholicism proved integral to my vocation. I wanted to be part of something greater than myself. My new-found faith had grabbed hold of me, but I had yet to realize it. Receiving Holy Communion with my classmates was just the tip of the iceberg.

I graduated eighth grade and headed to high school. I wandered away from going to Sunday Mass, but someone was watching. It was my grandma. When I was 15, she told me that I had to start going to Mass every Sunday. She was a lapsed Catholic, but every Sunday, she would drive me to church. She would not attend Mass but would wait outside for me sitting in the car. After Mass, she would go directly to our favorite diner, and we would have breakfast together. I loved it.

It was during this time that I began to think about the priesthood. I became quite zealous in studying and reading lots of material on Church history, the saints, and all things Catholic. However, when I finished high school I was still unsure of what direction to take.

I headed to college with the thoughts of the priesthood still there but not pronounced. I loved science and wanted to become a doctor. The career appealed to me because of secular reasoning: it was a prestigious profession and would allow me to have the finer things in life. I also believed that I would be a fine doctor. But after a year or so, the concept began to wear off. I realized that acquiring the material things in life was not important. As this awareness took hold, I started to embrace thoughts of the priesthood in a very positive way. I applied to and was accepted by the diocesan seminary in Richmond, Virginia. My journey to the Sacrament of Holy Orders had begun.

The diocesan priests were good and holy men. But I realized early on that something was missing. The diocesan priesthood did not fill the sense of camaraderie I was seeking. I knew my own temperament, and I needed a community structure to stay on the right path. Aristotle said long ago, "know thyself." I responded to his words.

During this discernment process, I went to my pastor and asked him if there was a directory or a phone book available with a listing of all the religious communities in it. The answer was yes! I was thrilled.

The book was like a "phone book" of religious orders everywhere. Included among them was the number for the Mercedarians. I had been praying for a "sign" from above to help me decide which path to take. Then I happened to be talking to the parish secretary, whose name was Peg. Peg said to me, "David, you have to be open to the little things God gives you."

She was right. I had been waiting for a sign that simply pointed me in the right direction. I had not paid attention to the "little things God was doing for me." A simple visit to the Mercedarians changed all that. I had found an Order of brothers on fire with the faith and in love with Jesus and his Church. This was a community of Catholic men with more than 800 years of unbroken history of tradition and faithfulness to the magisterium. They wore white habits and, besides taking the vows of chastity, poverty, and obedience, embraced a fourth vow. This is known as the redemptive vow. The friars willingly promise to exchange their lives for another if necessary to either save that person's mortal life or their spiritual life. The Order had a tremendous, *tremendous* history of saving souls. I knew I wanted to be part of this. I graduated college in May of 2005 with a bachelor's degree in science. That August, I entered the postulancy of the Order of Mercy. I was ordained to the priesthood in 2013.

I will finish by saying this: Becoming a Mercedarian was the best decision I made in my whole life.

Father David is on special assignment in Italy working on his Doctorate in Liturgy.

St. Raymond Nonnatus

Raymond Nonnatus came into the world in the year 1204. His birth was anything but ordinary. His mother died while she was giving birth to her son. While watching his wife die before his eyes, Raymond's father had the presence of mind to remove his unborn child from her womb with his own dagger in order to save his son's life. It is hard to imagine the emotions exploding in Raymond's father as he pulled his newborn son from his dead wife's abdomen.

He and his wife had already agreed to naming the child Raymond. However, the last name of Nonnatus may seem a bit strange. That is because it is Latin and it means "not born." Raymond became known as the child who was "not born."

Raymond's father owned several farms, and he wanted Raymond to manage one of them. But Raymond was drawn to religious life. He possessed a deep devotion to God and the Blessed Virgin. Nearby was the ancient chapel of St. Nicholas, and he would frequent there to pray and meditate. Eventually, his father realized that his son would not be a sheep-herder or farmer and gave in to the boy's wishes to join the Mercedarians.

Raymond's life was now on track for him to fulfill his God-given destiny. Empowered by his father's permission, Raymond told the Mercedarians that he had personally taken a vow of perpetual virginity and was determined to join the Mercedarian order. He was accepted, and legend has it that St. Peter Nolasco—the founder of the Mercedarians—is the one who presented Raymond with the Order's habit. The young man was likely ordained a priest in his early twenties, although there is some uncertainty about the exact date.

In 1224, Fr. Raymond began his first redemption journey to Valencia which the Moors had conquered. Father Raymond Nonnatus managed to gain the freedom of 233 captive Christians, but he was just beginning his work.

In 1226, he traveled to Algiers, in Northern Africa. Offering to remain behind as a replacement prisoner for the Moors, he freed another 140 captives. Three years later, he went back to Algiers again. This time he was accompanied by his friend, Friar Serapion.

Friar Serapion had fought alongside Richard the Lion-Hearted during the Crusades and became a Mercedarian. He had decided he would rather surrender his life for captives rather than kill infidels. The two of them managed to free 150 prisoners from slavery on that journey. In 1232, Raymond and Serapion managed to free 228 captives from the prisons and dungeons of Tunis.

Father Raymond's last redemption was in 1236. It was in Algiers again, and this visit is not known for the number of freed prisoners. Instead, it is known for the torture Fr. Raymond was forced to endure. Having exhausted all funds, Fr. Raymond stayed behind as a hostage. He spent his time in the dungeons preaching the message of Jesus and Christianity. Christian teachings were a bold refutation of the Muslim teachings, and his captors would have none of it.

Father Raymond was taken away, and they used a searing iron to bore holes through his upper and lower lips. Then they placed a padlock through the holes in an attempt to keep the suffering man quiet. The padlocks remained in place for eight months, until the ransom was received for Raymond's release. He was returned to Spain in 1239.

Raymond Nonnatus died toward the end of August 1240; the exact day is unknown. He was 36 years old. Tradition has it that the town, the local Count, and the friars all claimed his body. They resolved the dispute by placing Raymond's body across the back of a blind mule. The mule was let loose, and wherever it stopped would be Raymond's burial place.

The mule slowly ambled to the chapel where Raymond Nonnatus had prayed so frequently as a teenager. That is where he stopped, and that is where Raymond was buried. Since the 13th century, many miracles attributed to the intercession of Raymond Nonnatus have occurred at the site.

Saint Raymond Nonnatus was canonized a saint by Pope Alexander VII in 1657. He is the patron saint of childbirth, children, and pregnant women. He is also a patron for priests defending the seal of confession.

👑 *Feast Day. August 31*

Fr. Joseph Eddy O. de M.

F
ather Joseph Eddy was born in Montrose, Pennsylvania, in 1977. Montrose is a small town located in the northeastern part of the state between Binghampton, New York, and Scranton, Pennsylvania. Joseph had two older sisters, Maria and Theresa. He remembers how his mom was the guiding force in their traditional Catholic upbringing. From daily prayer to the family Rosary, to Sunday Mass, to being taught to "love your neighbor," their mom was their shining example. She even packed them in the car and drove them to confession on Saturday afternoons. Father Joseph would say that "Mom was the straw that stirred the brew."

In addition to instilling the solid core values of the Catholic faith and family life into her children, Joseph's mom also insisted that her kids become involved in a church activity. Young Joseph chose to become an altar server. It was somewhat providential that Joseph chose this ministry because his great-aunt worked in the rectory. She let Joseph come by and help her with her work, and the young man was able to spend time with the pastor who was often in the office. His early sense of being drawn to ministry probably began by being in contact with the Monsignor.

Mom instilled in her children a deep devotion to the Blessed Mother. This included praying the family Rosary most days during the week. They were encouraged to make morally correct choices and evaluate circumstances based on what they knew was right or wrong. By raising her children on a foundation of their Catholic faith, Mrs. Eddy had done her best to set her children on the path to a virtuous lifestyle.

Joseph began to feel the call to ministry grow while in high school. After graduation, he enrolled in Marywood University, a Catholic liberal arts college in Scranton, Pennsylvania. Marywood had been established in 1915 by the Sisters, Servants of the Immaculate Heart of Mary. Joseph would graduate with a bachelor of science degree in special education.

Joseph visited the Mercedarians in Philadelphia and felt immediately drawn to them. Inspired by their devotion to the Blessed Mother and their traditional embrace of the Catholic faith, Joseph applied and was accepted. It was not long after he would become a seminarian at St. Charles Borromeo Seminary in Wynnewood, Pennsylvania. In 2007, Joseph Eddy became a member of the Mercedarian Order when he was ordained a priest. He is now known as Fr. Joseph Eddy O. de M.

Besides being a priest, Fr. Eddy is also an experienced special education teacher, having started teaching before he became a priest. After ordination in 2007, he was appointed to the Vicariate Council for the Order and has served in that post since 2009. Father Eddy also worked within the Order as Moderator for the Secretariat of Religious Life.

Father Eddy is also one of the founding members of the Raymond Nonnatus Foundation for Freedom, Family, and Faith. He has been on the board of directors of the organization since 2015. He prays for and works with the families and individuals affected by divorce and separation.

He is also an avid sports enthusiast. His favorite teams include the Chicago Bears, the New York Yankees, Penn State Football, and Syracuse Basketball. But what makes Fr. Joseph Eddy happiest of all is serving Jesus and Mary as a Mercedarian friar. What follows is one of his stories of the vow of redemption in action.

It was about ten years ago when Fr. Joseph Eddy was stationed at the Mercedarian Vicariate located at the Monastery of Our Lady of Mercy in Philadelphia. This center served as the House of Formation for postulants and students. Candidates for the Mercedarian Order would begin their journey at this place. At the time, Fr. Eddy was Vocation Director and the Master of Postulants. Father also assisted at the parish whenever needed.

It was a weekday when Fr. Eddy was working at the parish office. A call came in and a man asked if he could speak to a priest. The receptionist at the desk asked the caller what kind of help he needed. The man said his wife was dying and she was asking for a priest. Father Eddy readily agreed to take the call.

He took the phone and said, "Hello, this is Fr. Eddy. How can I help you?"

The man began to speak, and he had a pronounced accent. Father interrupted the caller and said, "Excuse me, sir, could you speak a bit slower? I do not understand what you are saying."

The man slowly explained that he was calling for his wife, who had stopped practicing her faith when she married him. He was Hindu, and his name was Shivay. Neither of them practiced their respective religions. But his wife was dying with stage four pancreatic cancer, and she wanted to go back to her Catholic roots. She wanted to confess to a priest, receive the Sacrament of Anointing of the Sick, and receive Christ present in the Holy Eucharist. Father said, "Shivay, please tell me your wife's name?"

Shivay answered, "Her name is Sarah."

Father said, "Please tell Sarah I will be there in about an hour."

Shivay, in his heavy accent, replied, "Oh, thank you, Father, thank you. She be very happy. Thank you."

Shivay and Sarah lived in Bryn Mawr, a thirty- to forty-minute drive away. Father Eddy left about twenty minutes later. He headed west on I-76 and, within forty minutes, was pulling onto the gravel driveway. It had taken almost one hour from when he ended his phone call until he arrived at Shivay and Sarah's home

Father knocked on the door and waited a few minutes for someone to answer. Soon the door slowly opened and a small, thin man answered, dressed in a traditional Kurtu shirt looped around his neck. The man bowed slightly to the priest and said, "Hello, I am Shivay, Sarah's husband. Thank you so much for coming. She is very happy for you to come here. Please, come in."

As Shivay led Fr. Eddy over to his wife, she lifted her head from the pillow and let out a gasp. She said, "Oh my, you are Mercedarian. I cannot believe it." The dying woman was overjoyed.

Father Eddy was surprised at her reaction to him. "Hello, Sarah. So you know the Mercedarians? That is wonderful."

"Father, I was born in Buenos Aires and was taught by the Mercedarians in school. Of course, I know the Order. And I am so happy that a Mercedarian priest has come to me at this time in my life. It is the hand of God who sent you, Father."

Shivay, feeling a bit uncomfortable, said, "I go in other room and let you two talk. I wait till you call me back."

Sarah smiled at her husband and said, "Thank you, Shivay. Thanks to you, this has become a great day for me. I will call for you when we finish talking."

Father sat by Sarah's bedside, and they just talked. She told him how they had met 23 years earlier and that they had been married at the courthouse. Sarah said to Father, "We just wanted to be together but our families would not hear of it. So we just left our religious practices, got married by a judge at the court house, and that was that. We have been happy together, but not practicing our faith has been a black cloud hanging over each of us. It is time for me to ask God's forgiveness. After I am gone, I am not sure what Shivay will do. We have talked about it but he will have to decide himself. Maybe you can help him."

Sarah had not been to Mass in many years. She admitted to Fr. Eddy how much she did miss practicing her faith. She knew it was time to "make things right."

Father Eddy heard Sarah's confession. Then he anointed her forehead and the palms of her hands with holy oil blessed by the bishop during Holy Week. That was followed by her receiving Holy Communion. Then he gave her the Apostolic Pardon, an indulgence given to those close to death. It has the power to remit all temporal punishment due to sin. God's mercy is constantly being showered down upon us.

Sarah passed to her eternal reward that evening. It had been a wonderful day for her. Through the hands of his priest, God had embraced her with his love and forgiveness, and we can be assured that Jesus was waiting for her when she arrived at her everlasting home. Can't you just see him giving Sarah a big Jesus hug?

Father Joseph Eddy is presently with the Prison Ministry and an Adjunct Professor.

Servant of God Antonino Pisano

A ntonio Pisano was born in Cagliari, Italy, on the feast day of St. Joseph, March 19, 1907. He was the third of seven children of Stefano Pisano, a fisherman, and Raffaela Monni. His mom named her baby Antonio after her favorite saint, St. Anthony of Padua. The fishing industry did not provide enough work for Stefano to make a decent living and the family had little money. They even had to postpone the baptism until they saved enough of their meager funds to have the baptism.

They managed to have the baby baptized on April 7. Antonio came down with the measles soon after his birth and was sick for several months, at times bordering on death. Soon family and friends were lovingly calling him Antonino. His mother called on St. Anthony to cure her boy, and Antonino did recover.

Mamma Raffaela was a religious woman and did her best to educate her children in the faith. She made a point of instilling in them a great love for Our Blessed Lady and the saints. Antonino loved learning about the Blessed Mother and the saints and especially about Jesus. He would recreate the services he saw at church when he was home, making vestments to wear and using a table as an altar. His favorite game was called "run and catch." We know it as "tag."

In due time Papa Stefano Pisano was hired as a cellarman and soon was promoted to being a customs guard. The family's economic situation improved, and the Pisanos had to move. The first town was Sonnino when Antonino was seven. There would be another move, this one to Bonaria They moved onto the same street where the church of Our Lady of Bonaria was located. She had arrived there 544 years earlier, in 1370, floating up onto the shore in a wooden crate. The Mercedarians uncrated the miraculous statue and began the devotion to Our Lady and baby Jesus.

Antonino and his brother, Efisio, were enrolled in St. Louis Catholic School, in the Mercedarian monastery next door to the church. The school held both educational and recreational activities inside, and it was well-run. Father Luigi Spolverini liked Antonino and taught him how to be an altar boy. Antonino loved it, and every morning he was at the church well before the six-o'clock Mass began. He woke early to get to church and would wake everyone else up. His mom and dad decided he could go and stay with his Aunt Elena, his Godmother. She lived close to the church and was an early riser. In fact, she was happy to have Antonino sleeping over. She loved her Godson very much.

Some of Antonino's friends, along with Antonino's older brother, Efisio, were a bit jealous of him and picked on and bullied Antonino frequently. Efisio admitted to bullying Antonino but was amazed how his little brother would pray for him. Antonino would even light a candle for Efisio when he took a trip, praying for his safe return. His friends who bullied him also told the same thing about the frail Antonino. Years later, many would recall how Antonino was always forgiving.

On March 31, 1918, Antonino and his brother received their First Holy Communion together. Then on September 24, 1920, the Feast of Our Lady of Mercy, he received the Sacrament of Confirmation. He would go to confession frequently and go to Mass and receive Communion as often as possible. As time passed, Antonino realized that God was calling him to join the Mercedarians and give his life to Jesus and his Blessed Mother.

His mom told Fr. Luigi, who began the process for Antonino to join the Mercedarian Order. The young man filled out the application, which was accepted. On October 23, 1920, he entered the Mercedarian monastery as a postulant. He was 13 years old.

Things did not go smoothly for young Antonino. He was frail, and his vision was far from normal. His superiors scheduled him for several medical examinations, including one with an ophthalmologist. He diagnosed Antonino as having severe myopia, which meant he was extremely nearsighted. The doctor informed his superiors that it would be extremely difficult for the teenager to study and keep up with the others. Antonino was sent home. He told his mother, "One day, they will take me back."

His mother took him to another specialist who prescribed special reading glasses for him. The lenses were very thick, but they allowed him to study. Antonino was ecstatic and wanted to return to his religious life. He managed to do so but not with the Mercedarians. It was with the Capuchins. His Godmother had spoken to one of the Capuchin priests and asked if they would take her Godson. He talked to his superiors, and they agreed.

Antonino began his postulancy at the monastery of San Benedetto, where he worked hard and managed to get excellent grades and reviews. His superiors admired Antonino greatly and spoke of him often. Some other students became jealous and began tormenting their classmate. They accused him of things that were sinful, such as writing obscenities on the walls, desecrating the consecrated Host, and other untruths. Antonino never defended himself and they took advantage of that quiet trait he had. He was discharged from the Capuchin monastery. Ironically, three months later, the person that had orchestrated these vile acts against Antonino was discovered. Antonino's mother wanted him to go to the diocesan seminary, but Antonino desperately wanted to return to the Mercedarians. So his mom turned to Fr. Luigi, and he intervened for Antonino.

Since he could read and write and could do the necessary work, he was accepted back to the monastery of Bonaria. On February 10, 1922, he returned to the Mercedarians. His classmates were kind to him and helped him with his studies, especially mathematics which he struggled with. He kept working hard, and on March 5, 1922, he began his novitiate and donned the white habit of the Mercedarian order. On that occasion, Antonino, all of 15 years old, wrote the following prayer:

> *With the grace of the Lord and with the help of Mary Our Mother, I will abstain from any voluntary and felt sin or defect. But if by my misfortune I commit any of it, due to weakness or inadvertence, I will not lose courage, but after having repented and humbly asking for forgiveness, with the grace of God and with diligence and fervor, I will try to fulfill for the future always better my duties and to serve the Lord more faithfully.*

Antonino Pisano professed the three vows of poverty, chastity, and obedience on the Feast of the Immaculate Conception, December 8, 1923. He also promised the fourth vow of redemption, joyfully agreeing to give his life for another. He then began his theological studies in his quest to become a priest.

He had read the biography of St. Thérèse of the Child Jesus several times. The "Little Flower" had offered herself as a victim to merciful love. She was nineteen years old at the time. On the same page he had written his prayer, he also wrote a plea to St. Thérèse to help him with the grace to die before he was twenty-one.

Antonino developed a cold that did not go away. It advanced into a chronic cough, and many times he would develop a fever. Antonino fought through his illness as best he could and stayed committed to performing the duties required of him. This included assisting pilgrims who would come to honor Our Lady of Bonaria. One early May morning Antonino could not get out of bed. The doctors did not understand his high fever and took saliva samples. They discovered that Antonino had tuberculosis. He remained in bed in the monastery for three weeks and then transferred to a sanitarium. He believed his prayer to die before the age of twenty-one was being answered.

Antonino was sent home in the middle of July 1927. On August 6, 1927, surrounded by his family and his Mercedarian brothers, he shouted, "Do not cry, do not cry. I shall be back." Then he closed his eyes for the last time. He was twenty years old.

Antonino was initially buried in the cemetery next to the monastery. In 1938 he was moved into the sanctuary and placed in a niche near the chapel of the Crucifix. In 1958 he was once again moved, this time to a place near the main altar. Many people attributed prayers answered to Brother Antonino. His cause for sainthood was started, but World War II interrupted the process. It was restarted after the war and in 1957 Brother Antonino was elevated to Servant of God. His cause was then forwarded to Rome. It now is in the hands of the Congregation for the Causes of Saints.

PRAYER FOR THE BEATIFICATION OF
FRA ANTONINO PISANO, O. DE M.

O most glorious Virgin of Bonaria, who drew the angelic teenager Br. Antonino Pisano to your sanctuary and filled him with all the graces necessary for him to be a model for the youth, who are so threatened in our time. Grant that we may imitate his virtues and, if it please the Divine Master, may we obtain the grace of seeing him glorified in the Church so that he may be invoked with greater confidence. Amen.

To report any favors received through the intercession of Fra Antonino Pisana, please contact: segreteria@mercedari.it

Brother Raymond Colombaro O. de M.

My present life as a Mercedarian friar has its roots in the Third Order, the lay branch of our religious family. Looking for a more in-depth spirituality than my local parish was offering, I trolled around the internet looking for Third Orders in the Archdiocese of Philadelphia. Eventually I came upon a site for the Mercedarian Third Order whose members met at the Monastery of Our Lady of Mercy. I made a phone call and eventually met one of the two friars who were the spiritual directors of the group. This friar, Brother Matthew Levis, O. de M., kindly introduced me to the various members of the local chapter in September 2002.

I began coming to Masses and other liturgical events, meetings, and fundraisers sponsored by the Third Order, all of which were held at the Monastery of Our Lady of Mercy. Later that autumn, I made my first promises as a member of the Mercedarian Third Order. In May of 2003, those promises were finalized. As with every vocation story or life experience, there is the combination of comfort and challenge that comes with the territory.

By early December 2004, I found myself in a painfully untenable living situation and had recourse to the friars at the Monastery of Our Lady of Mercy. The Superior of the House, Fr. Matthew Phelan O. de M., graciously invited me to live at the Monastery as a guest until I could get on my feet.

Living in closer quarters with the friars became a pre-postulancy "program" of sorts, a mutual and "come and see" situation.

In February 2005, I contacted the friar who was the Vocation Director of the Vicariate of the United States, Fr. James Mayer O. de M. He recommended that I prayerfully consider becoming a member of the First Order as a Brother. Among the postulants living at the same time at the Monastery was [now] Fr. Scottston Brentwood O. de M., who gave me wise counsel during those early months of discernment.

After consulting with the Lord, a few close family members, and friends, I completed the application paperwork. My Mercedarian postulancy began in earnest on August 22, 2005, which fell on the feast of the Memorial of the Queenship of the Blessed Virgin Mary. As with every vocation story or life experience, the combination of comfort and challenge comes with the territory. Religious life is no different!

My "classmate" throughout religious formation was David Spencer. As Divine Providence would have it, my Mass of Solemn Profession took place on June 29, 2016, almost twelve years after David and I began our journey as classmates. Our paths separated as David moved on to study for the priesthood. On this day of my taking Solemn Vows, it was none other than Fr. David Spencer O. de M. who was the homilist.

What does it mean to me to be a Mercedarian? Moments of sheer joy as a Mercedarian friar happen when I see God in a child's laughter when the toddler and I are playfully enjoying one another's company. The same holds true in the seasoned wisdom of an aged person who shares a life experience with me.

Brother Raymond is presently on assignment as Sacristan at Our Lady of Mercy and St. Bridgid Parishes in Leroy, New York.

St. Serapion of Algiers

Saint Serapion of Algiers was born in 1179 in either England or Ireland. When he was a boy, his father took him along on the Crusades led by King Richard the Lion-Hearted. In 1191, at the age of twelve, he participated in the Battle of Acre. Here he met Peter Nolasco, who preached the mercy of God and did so by freeing Christian slaves from their Moorish captors. Serapion realized that the purpose of his life was to save lives, not to take them.

In 1222, Serapion became a full member of the Mercedarian order. He made several missions of mercy in northern Africa before being sent to England to recruit new members. During the journey, pirates attacked his ship, and he was left for dead. However, he survived and eventually made it to England. He began preaching against the theft of church property, and the authorities ordered him to leave the country.

In 1240, Serapion had gone to Algiers to secure the release of 87 Christian captives. However, the ransom he brought with him was not enough. The captors demanded more than Serapion had agreed on. When some prisoners heard this, they began to consider rejecting their Christian faith to save themselves. Serapion would not allow this to happen. He offered himself to the Moors in exchange for the prisoner's freedom. The Moors agreed, and Serapion watched as the prisoners were freed. He then knew it was time for him to begin preaching the love of God to his new captors.

Serapion had turned his very life over to his captors. Undaunted by his natural fear, he preached the love of God and the gospel message to the Muslims. Many began to respond to his message. However, as his brother Mercedarians hurried throughout Europe in the hope of gathering the extra ransom demanded, Serapion was making some hard-hearted enemies. When the Muslim leaders realized this Catholic Christian man was starting to convert his listeners, they turned against him.

Since the ransom had yet to arrive, the Muslim in charge ordered Serapion put to death. The man who wanted to preach the message about the God of love was crucified on an X-shaped cross. While still alive he was dismembered. The pain he endured must have been beyond description. Serapion died the proto-martyr of Algiers. Like his brother Mercedarians, St. Raymond Nonnatus and St. Peter Armengol, Serapion gave all he had—including his life—for the love of God.

Saint Serapion was beatified in 1625 by Pope Urban VIII and canonized by Pope Benedict XIII in 1728.

👑 *Feast Day: November 14*

Fr. Justin Freeman O. de M.

ather Justin Freeman was born in Warrenton, Virginia, in 1978. He grew up in a tiny village called Catlett. His dad, Frank, was a firefighter and his mom, Sue, was a nurse. They were people who served others. Frank and Sue had two children, and Justin was the oldest. His sister, Jennifer, was about a year and a half younger than her big brother.

Justin grew up on the family farm, and his only neighbors were his aunt and uncle. He loved to fish in the nearby pond and loved playing with the dogs, cats, and ducks that were the other farm residents. His family was Protestant and belonged to the Church of Christ.

When Justin was entering high school the family moved to the suburbs of Washington, D.C. In high school, Justin was active in the school orchestra, moved up through the ranks in the Boy Scouts, and eventually became an Eagle Scout. He also worked for Kentucky Fried Chicken.

Ironically, Justin knew he wanted to be a priest before becoming a Catholic. He converted to Catholicism at the age of 17.

Justin graduated high school and entered Longwood University in southern Virginia. While attending college, he was active in college in Model UN and was a member of the College Republican Club. He also served as president of the Political Science Club. Justin spent his junior year in Ireland as part of the foreign exchange program. When he returned home, he got a job working for the lobby firm of Preston Gates, which was founded by the father of Microsoft founder Bill Gates. He then attended the University of Dallas.

Prior to entering the seminary, he interned for the Social Security Administration and worked for the Republican National Committee. He also worked for a prominent lobbying firm in Washington, D.C. In 2004, Justin joined the Mercedarian Friars. He was ordained to the priesthood in 2010, becoming Fr. Justin Freeman O. de M. He holds master's degrees in divinity, theology, and political philosophy.

Father Freeman previously served as a chaplain of MetroHealth in Cleveland for five years and at parishes in the Dioceses of Buffalo and St. Petersburg. Father Freeman is presently Superior at the Monastery of Our Lady of Mercy in Philadelphia. In his free time, he enjoys reading and traveling.

Martyrs of the Spanish Civil War

D uring the bloody Spanish Civil War—which raged from 1936 through 1939—more than 6,800 clergy were murdered by the forces of the socialist Spanish government. Included among them were 19 Mercedarian friars from the Aragon province. Those Mercedarians who won the crown of martyrdom were: Mariano Alcalá, Tomás Carbonell, Francisco Gargallo, Manuel Sancho, José Trallero, Jaime Codina, Mariano Pina, Antonio Lahoz, Perdro Esteban, Tomás Campo, Francisco Llagostera, Serapio Sanz, Enrique Morante, Eduardo Massanet, Amancio Marín, Francisco Mitjá, Antonio González, Jose Reñé, and Lorenzo Moreno belonged to the communities of Barcelona, Lérida, El Olivar, and San Ramón.

They were not unaware of the hostile environment that was developing in those years, as demonstrated by expressions found in letters that they sent to their relatives. Blessed Jose Reñé wrote: "If we miss this opportunity, we will not have another."

In the words of Blessed Jaime Codina: "What a great gift to be a martyr; what glory! What good fortune!"

This environment of staunch witness that was experienced in the religious communities explains how, during the difficulties, there were no dissections from the faith and how, when they arrived at the final moment, they professed the name of Christ.

In his *Allocutio* address on September 14, 1936, Pope Pius XI put it this way:

"You are here, dearly beloved sons, to tell us about the great tribulation from which you have come out (Rev. 7:14); a tribulation of which you bear the visible marks and wounds on your persons and in your causes; marks and wounds of the great battle of sufferings that you have borne, having yourselves become a spectacle to our eyes and to those of the whole word (Hebrews 10:33); dispossessed and despoiled of everything, pursued and sought so as to be put to death in the cities and in the towns, in private homes and in the solitude of the mountains.

"You come to tell us about your joy for having been found worthy, like the first apostles, to suffer for the name of Jesus (Acts 5:41). All this is a splendid display of Christian and priestly virtues, of heroism and martyrdom; true martyrs in the full, sacred, and glorious meaning of the word, even to the sacrifice of the most innocent victims, of venerable elders, of those in the springtime of youth, even to the intrepid generosity that requests a place on the track with the victims who are awaiting the executioner.

"And the others? Nothing remains but to love them, and to love them with a special love of compassion and mercy."

Blessed Mariano and his companions—along with others—were beatified in the year 2014 in Tarragona, Spain.

♕ *Feast Day: September 16*

Fr. Oscar Z. Kozyra O. de M.

Zacarias Kozyra and Dominikia Bobyk were from Ukraine and belonged to the Byzantine Rite of the Catholic Church. As World War II loomed on the horizon, Zacarias decided it would be best to leave before the fighting began. They left Ukraine and emigrated to Argentina, settling in Buenos Aires. On September 26, 1945, Dominikia gave birth to a baby boy. They named him Oscar and he was baptized into the Byzantine rite on August 15, 1946. The Byzantine baptism rite includes administering the Sacraments of Confirmation and Holy Eucharist. The Holy Eucharist is placed on a small spoon and given to the child. Oscar received Holy Communion again in the Roman Rite on December 8, 1953.

Oscar credits his parents for planting the seeds for his vocation by their dedication to teaching him how to pray early in his life. Because of their diligence, Oscar could pray the Our Father, the Hail Mary, and the Glory Be in Ukrainian before the age of three. Oscar says that was the foundation for why he felt drawn to religious life.

Oscar's dad rarely went to church. He did go on Christmas and Easter but not other times. Oscar's mom occasionally took her boy to church and never really pressured her son to go. But Oscar's gift of faith was powerful, and he would go every week. Until the "incident."

When Oscar was eleven years old, he accidentally killed a cat. He does not even remember how it happened, but he knew he had to confess such a heinous act. He went to his church to confess. Hearing confessions was a young Spanish missionary priest. When Oscar revealed he had killed a cat, the priest grabbed him and began to shake him while yelling at him. Oscar was terrified and began to cry. He pulled away from the priest and ran from the church.

That night Oscar dreamed of the morning newspaper's headlines proclaiming his crime: "Oscar is a Cat Killer." Filled with fear, Oscar stopped going to church.

When Oscar was seventeen years old and in high school, a classmate asked him, "Are you Catholic?"Oscar told him that he was and then his friend asked him, "Well, why don't you go to church?" Oscar proceeded to tell his friend the story about the cat and the priest and how he shook Oscar and scared him so much that he ran away. His friend told him that would never happen again. He explained that the priest in question was long gone and that he should confess to the parish priest and tell him why he was gone so long.

Oscar did as his friend suggested and went back to his parish to confession. The older priest in the confessional was kind and gentle. The priest assured Oscar that Jesus was delighted that he had come back to Him. Oscar returned to Mass and the Sacraments, and from that point on, there was no looking back. He knew he wanted to be part of a religious order. He just was not sure which one.

Oscar was not drawn to any particular order. He investigated the Dominicans, the Jesuits, the Franciscans, and others. The Mercedarians won the day. He was drawn to the fourth vow, the redemptive vow, which helped him decide where he should be. On October 13, 1965, Oscar Kozyra joined the Mercedarian Order.

On February 15, 1966, Oscar entered the novitiate and made his first profession of vows one year later. Four years after that, on February 16, 1971, Oscar Kozyra made his solemn profession of vows.

Oscar was nearing the end of his journey and was ordained to the transitional diaconate on December 22, 1971. Two years later, on May 6, 1973, the Fourth Sunday of Easter, Oscar Kozyra was ordained to the priesthood by His Eminence, Raul Francisco Cardinal Primatesta, the Archbishop of Cordoba, Argentina. He would be forever known as Father (Friar) Oscar Z. Kozyra O. de M.

Father Oscar had a desire to go to Africa as a missionary. However, his bishop refused his request telling Fr. Oscar that he was not ready for such a challenging assignment in such a harsh environment. He would need more experience first. The bishop did tell him he would allow him to go to India as a missionary. And so, in early 1985, Fr. Oscar Kozyra O. de M. left for India to work with the poor, sick, and homeless. Father Oscar was getting acclimated to the culture, environment, and people within his jurisdiction. The sisters were there to help him better understand the natives and their customs. Then came his accident.

It was about three o'clock in the morning when Fr. Oscar decided to take a shower. While stepping from the stall, he slipped. As his feet flew outward and up, his torso straightened. The fall was fast and hard. Father landed on a ridge of tiles, his lower back taking the brunt of the fall. He had broken part of his lower back and could barely move. They managed to get him to the hospital, where he would remain for the next several weeks.

When Fr. Oscar was able to travel, the Order had him transferred to Rome. It was the end of 1987. The Order assigned him to St. Susannah's Church, the National Church of the United States in Rome. He would remain in Rome until 1995.

Sometime in 1995, Fr. Oscar Kozyra boarded a plane in Rome and hours later landed in Boston. He then traveled to Cleveland, Ohio, the home base for the Mercedarians in America. He had been sent to the United States because he spoke fluent Spanish. One month later, he was flown to Tampa, Florida, and then driven across Tampa Bay to the Mercedarian Center located in St. Petersburg, Florida. It was known as the St. Peter Nolasco House. It was adjacent to the Cathedral of St. Jude the Apostle, the center of the Diocese of St. Petersburg.

Father would say Mass and hear confessions at St. Jude's and other parishes in the area. He would conduct devotions and be available for Spanish-speaking assignments. After 37 years, Fr. Oscar Kozyra O. de M. is still serving in the Diocese of St. Petersburg. He resides at Nolasco House in St. Petersburg, Florida. He has been a priest for fifty years.

Kevin Cush
Mercedarian Postulant

K evin Cush is a postulant. What does that mean? It simply means he is a beginner. He has been accepted into the Mercedarian Order and completed his first year living in community. This was the Monastery of Our Lady of Mercy in Philadelphia. But before this all happened, there was a personal journey taken by Kevin. Some call this a period of discernment. This means that during the previous several years Kevin has prayed and thought hard about what path he wanted to take in life.

Kevin's discernment journey had taken him to a point where he knew for sure he wanted a life of serving God and others. He had now taken the step of committing to the Mercedarian Order. He liked their life in community and the work they did. However, we should explore Kevin's childhood and teenage years and learn how his early life led him to the Monastery of Our Lady of Mercy.

Kevin Cush was born in Cleveland, Ohio, and was the only child of Brian and Jennifer Cush. Kevin never attended Catholic school but spent all of his school years in public school right through high school and college. His Catholic faith was taught entirely to him by his mom and grandparents.

Kevin's mom was a devout Catholic as were her parents. Sunday Mass was a fact of life in the Cush house and Kevin received the Sacraments of First Holy Communion and Confirmation as a young boy. After that, he started attending daily Mass with his grandpa. In fact, one of Kevin's earliest memories is that of praying the Rosary with his grandfather. Kevin says, "Seeing the example set by my family and the inspiration it gave me was important in my Catholic upbringing because it helped me understand the beauty of the faith."

Kevin remembers that it was during early childhood and after attending daily Mass with his grandpa that he first had thoughts about becoming a priest. He said. "something stirred inside me, and I could feel God calling. I also felt that call while I was going to high school."

As a teenager, Kevin was attracted to girls. He had several girls he was close with but did not date much. He believed what held him back was that he always had the priesthood on his mind and that he never considered marriage.

Kevin got his driver's license when he reached the age of 16. This may have been providential because this was how he found the Mercedarians. Besides driving to school every day, Kevin had an earlier stop he would make. He would drive to Our Lady of Mt. Carmel Church on Detroit Avenue in Cleveland. This parish was home to the Mercedarians, including the Mercedarian Sisters of the Blessed Sacrament. There was a Mass at six-thirty every morning, and Kevin could still be on time for the start of his first-period class. It was here where he got his first exposure to both the friars and the sisters at work. Seeing them busy in and around the parish attracted him to the Mercedarian Order.

Following high school, Kevin entered the college seminary for the Diocese of Cleveland. There, he realized God was calling him to religious life, which was quite different from the diocesan priesthood. After a year he left there and finished his undergraduate degree at the local college.

Kevin explains, "Many people may not understand the difference between a diocesan priest and a friar in a religious order. One of the primary differences is just the lived-out experience; friars and religious tend to live in community. For diocesan priests, that might not be the same. Also, a diocesan priest makes promises on the day of his ordination. For a religious, long before he is ordained, there are professions and religious vows of poverty, chastity, and obedience. The Mercedarians also take a fourth vow. It is called the Vow of Redemption. Mercedarians vow to offer themselves for those who risk losing their faith, including sacrificing their lives if necessary. These vows come long before ordination to the priesthood."

The final thing that made Kevin choose the Mercedarians was, "Above all, the devotion and complete entrustment of our Order to Mary. That was the essential characteristic for me. We view Our Lady as the foundress of our Order. Giving our entire lives to Mary in service was something that was essential."

Postulant Kevin Cash began his journey in 2021. He successfully finished his first year and moved to the Charles Borromeo Seminary in Philadelphia. He lived at the Monastery of Our Lady of Mercy, also in Philadelphia. Kevin received his habit in September of 2022 while in San Ramon, Barcelona, Spain. He made his first simple vows on August 22, 2023.

Brother Kevin says, "I think one of the greatest joys of living in community is the communal prayer. Coming together several times throughout the day to pray as a community and afterward, having a meal or some recreation together is very special because it's not just the prayer, and it's not just living together. It is the combination that brings a lot of joy and makes communal life special."

Does Kevin have any advice for other young men discerning their vocation, whether it is to marriage, religious life, or priesthood?

"I would say number one is to trust God There is no kind of magical way or process or some kind of secret knowledge that you have to find in order to obtain your vocation. To trust God more than anything that he will have you be where He wants you to be. Do not be anxious about your vocation, but to view your vocation as an act of love and service to the Church."

He is presently known as Brother Kevin Cash O. de M. and resides at the Holy Family Mercedarian House of Studies in Columbus, Ohio. Here he attends the Pontifical College Josephinum where he studies for the priesthood.

Fr. James Mayer O. de M.

F ather James Mayer O. de M. looks back on his life as one filled with simplicity. He was the oldest of two boys born to non-Italian parents who had moved into an all-Italian neighborhood in Cleveland, Ohio. Naturally, their home was located in an all-Italian parish. Its name was St. Rocco's, and it was founded in 1914.

The year was 1970, and the neighborhood was changing. St. Rocco's had a Catholic school, including kindergarten. None of the other Catholic schools in the city had one. James and Audrey Mayer wanted their children to attend a Catholic kindergarten. James, as the oldest, became his parents' litmus test. Mom and dad enrolled him in St. Rocco's, and that is where it all began for five-year-old James Mayer.

The Mayers had been welcomed to the parish by a Mercedarian priest, Fr. Andrew Costanzo. Father Costanzo was the pastor of St. Rocco's at the time and his warm and friendly manner helped make Jim and Audrey feel right at home. Audrey quickly became active in the PTA, different sodalities, and many other church functions. James's dad was forever grateful to Fr. Andrew for making them feel right at home at St. Rocco's. James has said that he believes that if Fr. Andrew had not reached out to the family the way he did, things would never have worked out the way they did.

The teachers in the school, including kindergarten, were religious sisters. However, the friars were always around. They would be seen in the school hallways, walking outside in the courtyard, and creating a memorable presence in the atmosphere of St. Rocco's. James and the other kids especially loved Brother Richard Henry. He was a huge man, and when you are five years old, it was like standing next to a giant.

Brother Richard's size was not threatening to any of the children. That was because his kind and gentle manner shined through to all around him, and he became a "big teddy bear." As for James Mayer, he was always attracted to the friars and the life they lived. He especially enjoyed talking to them. There was never a reason not to approach them. The kids were never afraid of them because, like Brother Richard, they were easy to talk to and all were kind and friendly.

Brother Richard did do one thing the other friars did not. Occasionally he would give the kids Our Lady of Mercy medals. James always kept his.

James's family—from his mom and dad, to his grandparents, aunts, uncles, cousins, and other relatives—were all part of a deeply ingrained Catholic culture. Naturally, James and his brother became altar servers. They would ride their bicycles around the neighborhood and, more often than not, wind up at St. Rocco's. They would get involved in helping out one way or another and became a part of the parish family.

During his high school years, James began to think about whether or not he had a vocation. He wondered if God was reaching out and calling him. The teenager started giving serious thought to the possibility of a calling to religious life. He was in a Catholic high school in Cleveland, Ohio, and Catholicism had been part of him since his formative years. But he was not sure how to proceed. So he turned to prayer.

His prayers led him to the Holy Spirit, who, in turn, led him to Fr. Mark Hollis, the chaplain of Holy Name High School. Father Hollis helped James begin his discernment process. James was sure he did not want to be a priest. He wanted to be a religious brother. He felt called to that life.

A family friend, Fr. John Kreegan, was a diocesan priest in the Cleveland Diocese, the same as Fr. Hollis. They joined together, combining forces trying to steer James into giving the most serious consideration of entering the diocesan seminary of Cleveland, and studying to be a diocesan priest. But James was not sure.

The time frame was in the late 1970's and early 1980's. Diocesan priests were increasingly living alone as the number of priestly candidates kept decreasing. James knew he would miss family life. His discernment process had hit a road block.

James kept thinking about how he would miss being part of a family. He had seen how the Mercedarian friars lived. He saw how the young friars—students at the time—would come to St. Rocco's during Easter and summertime to work at the parish. He loved how they would go out together to a movie or a baseball game or just out for ice cream. That lifestyle appealed to him. The direction he would take was becoming more apparent to him.

During the summer of his senior year in high school, James's mom and her friend drove him to Philadelphia to visit the Mercedarians. He was not yet 18, and his mother had to sign papers for him to begin the application process. James was, as the saying goes, "gung-ho."

Life has a way of placing roadblocks and obstacles in our way as we journey forward. During his senior year of high school, James's grandmother and some other close relatives passed away. For the family, it was an emotionally difficult time. James put things on hold for a year. He worked at K-Mart, and he loved it. He also began doing janitorial work at St. Rocco's and entered the community college. He kept busy working and enjoying time with family and friends for the year.

The year passed, and James knew it was time to embrace his discernment results and move forward. He reapplied with the Mercedarians. There was a difference. His call to the brotherhood had changed. James Mayer was answering the call to the holy priesthood.

James Mayer began his studies in Philadelphia in 1984 at the formation house on Drexel Road. He spent the next seven years in Philadelphia studying at St. Charles Borromeo seminary.

James completed his studies and passed through his novitiate. He made his vows, and the Order sent him to Rome. Once there, he completed his studies in theology and earned his licentiate, which confirms he is qualified to be a theologian.

On December 5, 1992, James and Audrey Mayer boarded a plane in Cleveland, Ohio. They were about to take their first overseas flight. As the plane cleared the runway, they began to loosen the grip they had on each other's hands. They looked at each other and smiled. They were traveling to Rome for the ordination of their son. Brother James Mayer was being elevated to the sacred Order of the Diaconate. James remembers how his hands were sweating as he processed toward the church, even though there was a chill in the air. As his proud parents looked on, Brother James and a Mercedarian from Italy named Brother Rosario were ordained to the Diaconate. Most Reverend Joseph Mani, Auxiliary Bishop of Rome, officiated.

The church was filled to capacity, and the beautiful singing from the choir was inspiring. He remembers how a sudden sense of calm and peace filled him. His only concern was that he would not make the proper Italian responses to Bishop Mani's questions. The Bishop, a kind and gentle man, put both men at ease. Everything went perfectly.

After the service, an outdoor reception was held. Deacon James and Deacon Rosario were physically lifted into the air by parishioners, and the crowd yelled out, "Auguri!" "Auguri!" which means "congratulations!"

Later on in the day, the newly ordained and their guests celebrated at a feast prepared by a Mercedarian brother and his sister. Fellow Mercedarians served the meal, and it was fabulous. At the time, Deacon James reflected how "it was a beautiful and moving day that brought me closer to the fulfillment of my dreams. It was a day I will never forget."

On July 31, 1993, Deacon James Mayer was ordained to the most Holy Priesthood in the parish where it all began, St. Rocco's in Cleveland, Ohio. From that day on he would always be known as Fr. James Mayer O. de M.

Today Fr. James Mayer is the pastor of St. Rocco's Catholic Church in Cleveland. He was appointed to that post on April 11, 2016. He also has spearheaded a program modeled after Alpha, an organization that evangelizes those who have fallen away from the faith or have never heard of Jesus.

Our Lady of Mercy: Mother and Foundress of the Order of the Blessed Virgin Mary of Mercy

Along with the Church, the Mercedarian Order admires and exalts Mary, who is united to the saving work of her Son by an indissoluble bond. She is the most splendid fruit of redemption, and they contemplate her as the purest image of that which all members yearn and hope to be.

The Mercedarians intend to love Mary as her sons and to honor her as their "Mother", for she is the spiritual foundress of the Order. They strive to uphold her as a lively model of consecration to God and of redemptive service to men. They beg her constantly for faithful perseverance in their vocation and feel obliged to promote with ardor her devotion among members of the Mercedarian family and oppressed Christians and the faithful entrusted to their apostolic service.

In order to know and imitate her better, the Mercedarians study with particular interest who Mary is as a person. They must show forth her mission and the privileges with simplicity and competence and promote authentic Marian devotion by their life and example.

Mercedarians honor the Mother of God especially with the following acts:

- Daily, the recitation of five decades of the Rosary.
- On Saturdays, according to liturgical law, celebration of the Mass of our Most Holy Mother and the Liturgy of the Hours of the Blessed Virgin Mary; and, at the appropriate hour, the singing of the "Salve Regina."
- On the last Saturday on each month, special prayers for oppressed Christians.
- On September 24, the solemn celebration of her feast.
- The dedication of provinces, churches, and oratories to the Blessed Virgin Mary.
- The presence of the image of the Blessed Virgin Mary in the choir and private rooms of the religious.

♕ *Feast Day: September 24*

Mercedarian Vocation Overview

MISSION

The Order of the Blessed Virgin Mary of Mercy, founded in 1218, is an international community of priests and brothers, who live a life of prayer and communal fraternity based on the Rule of St. Augustine and the constitutions of the order. From this life flows the apostolic work of the order that seeks to carry on the work of our founder, St. Peter Nolasco, who in imitation of Jesus the Redeemer, offered his life for those Christians in need of redemptive love. The Mercedarians serve in schools, prisons, hospitals, and foreign missions. Today they assist those who are captive and oppressed by the problems of modern life.

QUALIFICATIONS

Candidates must be a Roman Catholic man, in good health and moral standing, who has earned at least a high school diploma, and who knows that the greatest love one can give is the gift of his own life completely, in exchange for the life and freedom of Christians in danger of losing their faith.

FORMATION

Discernment: During this time the director communicates with the individual in understanding the Mercedarian life and spirit.

Postulancy: This period lasts no less than nine months and extends until the novitiate begins. During this time the postulant lives with the religious community at the Monastery of Our Lady of Mercy in Philadelphia, Pennsylvania, and fully takes part in the spiritual and communal life of the friars which includes prayer, meditation, Holy Mass, recreation and their apostolate. In addition, there are weekly catechism classes.

Novitiate: The novitiate is one year, during which the novice deepens and intensifies his love for Jesus and the Mercedarian religious life through study, prayer and meditation.

Simple profession: This is a period lasting three to six years during which the professed renews his vows annually. At this time he attends a nearby Catholic university or local seminary. A friar candidate for the priesthood will attend philosophy and theology classes at the University of Salamanca in Spain, and the Gregorianum in Rome, Italy. A friar who is a brother will begin his studies in an area in which he is talented and that can be used within the order's apostolic work. For example: education, social work, prison or hospital ministries.

Solemn profession: After the solemn profession of vows, the friar completes his formation to the Mercedarian life and begins full time ministry.

SPIRITUALITY

What is spirituality? In our times, spirituality is falsely mistaken as a substitute for religion. However, nothing could be further from the truth! True spirituality is how we, as Catholics, live out our baptismal consecration through both prayer and action. In the religious life, this takes on an added element of total consecration to God through the vows of chastity, poverty, and obedience. For the Mercedarian, however, seeking out the perfection of charity goes further, their spirituality is enlivened by their fourth vow. Therefore, in all that they do—prayer, work, rest, exercise, or study—Mercedarians do it all for the captives.

It is no accident that the elements of Mercedarian spirituality can be envisioned as the very same emblem which each friar proudly wears upon his habit. These elements form the basis of their approach to love of God and neighbor as St. Peter Nolasco, their Founder did, over 800 years ago! The elements that distinguish their particular spirituality from other religious orders and congregations are:

• Redemptive Charity, or, rather love to the point of heroism;

• Imitation of Christ the Redeemer;

• Filial love and devotion to our Blessed Mother;

• Mercy; and,

• Prayer and devotion to Christ in the Eucharist.

Prayer Life

Each Mercedarian community establishes the time and manner of prayer and of the other community devotion and submits all to the approval of the Provincial. The Superior, as the spiritual promoter of the community, takes care of their daily fulfillment as well as the celebrations set forth in the ritual for the feasts of the Order. Mercedarians observe:

• Daily celebration or participation in the Eucharistic liturgy;

• Daily recitation of the Liturgy of the Hours, especially Morning Prayer and Evening Prayer, in common;

• Daily recitation of five decades of the Rosary, in common;

• Daily visitation to Our Lord in the Blessed Sacrament;

• Daily time spent in mental prayer;

• Adoration of the Lord in the Blessed Sacrament with a weekly Holy Hour.

Today, the Order of the Blessed Virgin Mary of Mercy is a worldwide organization. They continue rescuing people from attacks on their faith. Although located in 17 countries, there is only a small contingent of Mercedarian Friars working in the United States. At the present time they have locations in Philadelphia, Pennsylvania; Cleveland and Columbus, Ohio; and Leroy, New York. Their student house is in Philadelphia. They can be found working in deprived neighborhoods, in hospitals among drug addicts, and with families through parish work. The Mercedarians are a shining example to all Catholic Christians the world over.

THE WHITE SCAPULAR & THE MERCEDARIAN THIRD ORDER

Scapulars began showing up in the Middle Ages. They were used as a way of identifying a certain religious group to which a person felt connected. While the most popular color scapular is the brown scapular which represents Our Lady of Mt. Carmel, the white scapular represents the Mercedarians. From the very beginning, the Mercedarian Scapular was an outward sign of one's devotion to the Blessed Virgin Mary and of her call to work for captive Christians. Our Lady wore white and the habits worn by the Mercedarians are also white with the shield of the Order on the front. Third Order Mercedarians, made up of members of the laity, also wear the white scapular as they are an integral part of the redemptive mission. This allows them to share in the spiritual benefits of the Order.

Epilogue

After its founding, the Order of Mercy spread rapidly throughout Europe. But it was not until the late 15th Century that their presence spread across the great Atlantic Ocean. Christopher Columbus brought the first Friars to America on his second voyage, which set sail on October 13, 1493. The Mercedarians quickly established convents in Mexico, Cuba, Ecuador, Brazil, Chile, and Peru. It was not until the 20th Century that the Mercedarians made it into the United States.

Today, the Order of Mercy friars focus their rescue on those held captive by the modern world's invisible chains. These include the social, political, physical, and psychological prisons, such as drugs, homelessness, illness, incarceration, divorce, and addictions to other vices. They also assist in schools and parishes, a prime part of their ministry in the United States.

Please remember that the Order of the Blessed Virgin Mary of Mercy wants to shout out to Americans, "Hey folks, we are here. We come to serve. We are the Mercedarians."

The purpose of this book was to inform you, the reader, about the Mercedarians, specifically those working in the United States. Hopefully, introducing you to the Mercedarians will encourage your interest. The Mercedarian friars, nuns, and tertiaries are amazing, grace-filled people willing to trade their own lives to save others. Are you called to join them? Prayerfully you will take the next step by visiting their website or sending an email asking one question: "Can you please tell me more?"

Contacts

U. S. VICARIATE HEADQUARTERS

Monastery of Our Lady of Mercy
6398 Drexel Road
Philadelphia, PA 19151-2596
(215)879-0594

WEBSITE

www.orderofmercy.org

MERCEDARIAN FRIARS USA VOCATION OFFICE

584 W Broad Street
Columbus, OH 45215-2710

vocations@ordercfmercy.org

VOCATION DIRECTOR

Father Daniel Bowen, O. de M.
frdanielbowen@gmail.com

FACEBOOK

MercedarianFriarsUSA

X (FORMERLY TWITTER)

@4thvow

INSTAGRAM

mercedarianfriarsusa

YOUTUBE

@MercedarianFriarsUSA

MERCEDARIAN THIRD ORDER:

mlf.merced@gmail.com

The most important thing we do in life is to die well.

For those who are suffering, dying, as well as those who attend to them, this is a time that can be very difficult.

Beautifully designed and thoughtfully curated, *Passing Time* is a treasury of over 300 pages of classical Catholic texts to help people who are going through this time of life. It has catechesis, meditations, and prayers on suffering, the hour of death, mourning and burial, and Purgatory and remembrance.

 www.catholictreehouse.com/passing-time

Enflame your love for the Sacred Heart of Jesus

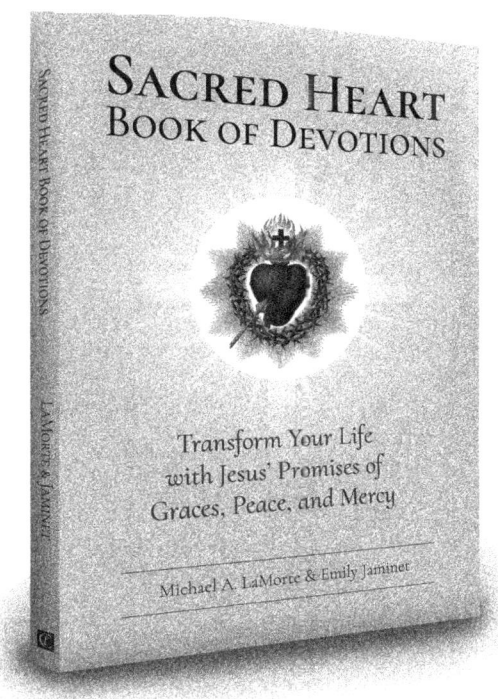

Perhaps the most comprehensive Sacred Heart devotional to date, the *Sacred Heart Book of Devotions* is a timeless collection of essential resources. Full of history, timeless prayers and novenas, classical sacred art, hymns, and more, this is an incredible resource for anyone who has or wants to develop a devotion to the Sacred Heart.

---

www.catholictreehouse.com/sacred-heart

Want to put your faith into action?
Let the saints show you how.

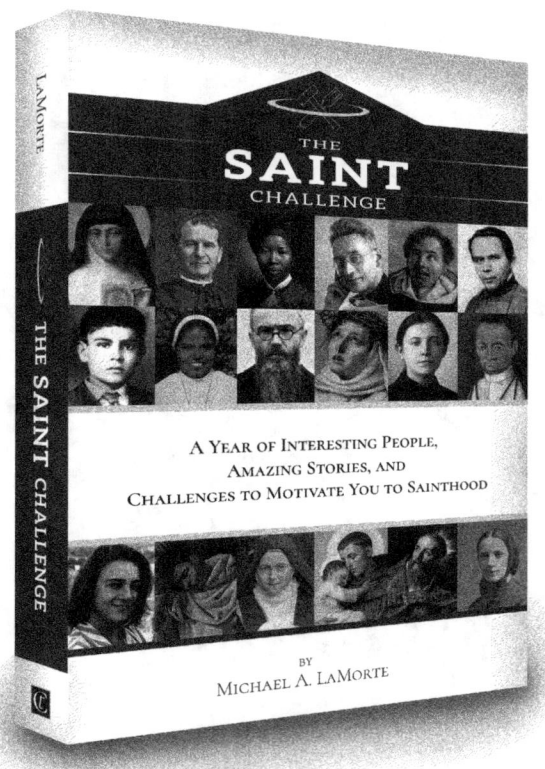

The Saint Challenge is a daily devotional that brings the saints alive and puts your faith to work inspired by their example. Designed to be used over and over, *The Saint Challenge* offers you a unique opportunity to delve into the captivating lives of the saints to find wisdom and inspiration for your own journey of faith. Over 450 pages of stories, challenges, and resources that turn the witness of their lives into inspiration for your personal growth in holiness.

www.thesaintchallenge.com

www.ingramcontent.com/pod-product-compliance
Lightning Source LLC
Chambersburg PA
CBHW060527130626
46553CB00002B/674